## BUILDING YOUR BRAND IN THE EXPERIENCE ECONOMY

# JÖRG DIETZEL

Copyright © 2020 Jörg Dietzel

Published by Marshall Cavendish Business
An imprint of Marshall Cavendish International

All rights reserved

No part of this publication may be reproduced, stored in a retrieval system or transmitted, in any form or by any means, electronic, mechanical, photocopying, recording or otherwise, without the prior permission of the copyright owner. Requests for permission should be addressed to the Publisher, Marshall Cavendish International (Asia) Private Limited, 1 New Industrial Road, Singapore 536196. Tel: (65) 6213 9300 E-mail: genref@sg.marshallcavendish.com
Website: www.marshallcavendish.com/genref

The publisher makes no representation or warranties with respect to the contents of this book, and specifically disclaims any implied warranties or merchantability or fitness for any particular purpose, and shall in no event be liable for any loss of profit or any other commercial damage, including but not limited to special, incidental, consequential, or other damages.

Other Marshall Cavendish Offices:
Marshall Cavendish Corporation, 99 White Plains Road, Tarrytown NY 10591-9001, USA • Marshall Cavendish International (Thailand) Co Ltd, 253 Asoke, 12th Floor, Sukhumvit 21 Road, Klongtoey Nua, Wattana, Bangkok 10110, Thailand • Marshall Cavendish (Malaysia) Sdn Bhd, Times Subang, Lot 46, Subang Hi-Tech Industrial Park, Batu Tiga, 40000 Shah Alam, Selangor Darul Ehsan, Malaysia.

Marshall Cavendish is a registered trademark of Times Publishing Limited

**National Library Board, Singapore Cataloguing-in-Publication Data**

Name: Dietzel, Jörg.
Title: Touch : building your brand in the experience economy / Jörg Dietzel.
Description: Singapore : Marshall Cavendish Business, [2020]
Identifier(s): OCN 1133229845 | ISBN 978-981-4868-52-5 (paperback)
Subject(s): LCSH: Branding (Marketing) | Advertising. | Communication in marketing.
Classification: DDC 658.827--dc23

Printed in Singapore

Cover illustration: Freepik.com

For Klaus Dietzel (1937–2013)

# ACKNOWLEDGEMENTS

I am much indebted to PingPing Han, who helped to bring the experience economy idea to life for our talk at Singapore Management University (SMU).

At the university, I am grateful to Professor Francis Koh, who first hired me many years ago, and to Professor Michelle Lee and Professor Jin Kyung Han, who welcomed me back. Dr Lim Lai Cheng at SMU Academy saw potential in me to share my experiences with her SkillsFuture classes. Sam Wu for always having my back. Also to the brands I have had the privilege to meet or even work with over time – many of them have found their way into this book.

Thank you to my previous and current students who – through their enthusiasm and participation – create an inspiring learning experience for me every week.

My good kaki Muhammad Al Khatieb (Memet) helped make sure we received the materials we needed from the brands selected, in his own friendly way. I couldn't have done this without you.

Thank you to Clarence Singham for your wise counsel, and to Nathan Goh for continuously challenging me to look at life in a new light. And Melvin Neo at Marshall Cavendish went from editor to good friend, gently nudging for delivery and always believing that I still have a few books in me.

Thank you to my mum Margret Dietzel, who – reluctantly – let me go out into the world, again and again, knowing this is what I needed to do.

Finally, I thank Singapore, my chosen home, for accepting me as one of your own.

# CONTENTS

**PREFACE**   9

**INTRODUCTION**   13

CHAPTER 1   **THE BESPOKE EXPERIENCE**   17

CHAPTER 2   **THE SOCIAL EXPERIENCE**   29

CHAPTER 3   **THE EVENT EXPERIENCE**   39

CHAPTER 4   **THE BRICK-AND-MORTAR SHOP EXPERIENCE**   53

CHAPTER 5   **THE HERITAGE EXPERIENCE**   71

CHAPTER 6   **THE CULTURAL EXPERIENCE**   81

CHAPTER 7   **THE SERVICE EXPERIENCE**   107

CHAPTER 8   **THE DIGITAL EXPERIENCE**   119

CHAPTER 9   **THE OVERALL BRAND EXPERIENCE**   131

CHAPTER 10   **EXPERIENCES AND CULTURAL MOMENTS**   145

**ABOUT THE AUTHOR**   151

# PREFACE

I have always been interested in people, brands and experiences.

From a young age, our house was open for guests from India to Africa, the Americas to Asia; "club friends" from a charitable international organization my parents were volunteers in.

I remember, as soon as I had picked up some English, sitting behind the living room door with my sisters, listening to the conversations, lapping up the tales from faraway lands, of orphans saved and money raised. I knew there was a big, interesting world out there, just waiting to be explored by me.

My journeys began when I was 12. My parents put me on a plane to the UK, on my own, for the summer holidays. A few years later, when I was 16, it was California, USA. I remember landing at LAX (Los Angeles Airport) after a long flight with nobody to pick me up (the dog had scared away the telegram courier informing my hosts of my departure) on the 4th of July 1978, only to spend literally all of my traveller's cheques that were supposed to last me for six weeks on a single cab ride to Simi Valley. During my studies in the then German capital city of Bonn, some part-time work in journalism and public relations took me first to Liverpool. There I wrote about the 1983 UK election campaign – my report was called "Watching the elephant die". Then off I went to Bali, accompanying the ballroom dancing world champions on their tour of Asia.

Experiences fascinated me – the more foreign, the better. So I was happy to receive a post-graduate research scholarship to spend a year studying in Durban, South Africa, in 1988. During my year there, I did anything but study – from trips to Stellenbosch to speak at their University, to Swakopmund in Namibia, term breaks spent on farms in Zimbabwe, or daytrips with our local Bible fellowship up-coast to Zululand and the Drakensberg. I created my own experiences.

As expected, work then led me from Germany to London, Beijing, Berlin, Singapore, Hong Kong and Korea. In 2019, I returned to Singapore, my home of choice.

The advertising agencies and marketing departments I worked with over the past 25 years or so were in the business of creating experiences for their clients' brands. These ranged from emotional TV commercials to memorable events. Later there were Instagram stories of island trips (for Audi), concerts, exhibitions and an ambitious coffee-table-book magazine.

It was in mid 2019 that the Singapore Management University, where I have taught since 2005, asked me to

PREFACE 11

Exhibition in Korea showcasing Audi Magazine.

present a talk to their alumni. They wanted something on branding, featuring a business started by an alumnus. I immediately thought of my friend PingPing at Culturally.co, and during discussions we both realised the urgency of the topic. It instinctively felt right, and first a talk and then this book were born.

When selecting the case studies for the different areas of the experience economy I looked at a mix of brands that I was familiar with, with somewhat of a focus on Asia. Because, having lived here since 1998 (with one brief intermezzo at Audi Global HQ), I do believe that the future is Asian in services and tech, travel and political power, healthcare, manufacturing and, yes, experiences.

# INTRODUCTION

The Experience Economy is not exactly new. More than 20 years ago, B. Joseph Pine II and James Gilmore coined the phrase in an article in the *Harvard Business Review*\*.

But the arrival of the internet, and especially of social media, has given the term a new life. These days, we are no longer using expensive brands to impress our peers and neighbours (at least in developed markets) as much as before. Instead we trek through the Kalahari or dive with sharks in Gansbaai, as long as we get to post a video of our experience on Instagram.

Experiences, particularly when shared online, have become the new currency. All around the world, consumers are using social media to share not just the trips they make, but also the food they eat, the fashion they wear and the adorable first steps of their baby.

So how is that important for brands? Brands, which yesterday were still striving to become status symbols to

\* Pine, B. Joseph II and Gilmore, James, "Welcome to the Experience Economy," *Harvard Business Review*, July 1, 1998.

command a higher price and encourage word-of-mouth (especially in those hard-to-reach places like messenger apps conversations, now weirdly called "Dark Social"), can use the quest for experiences by turning themselves into Experience Brands. The understanding of some global trends – from the search for individuality to the need for social engagement and the importance of values for millennials – can help brands differentiate and position themselves as the perfect solution for consumers' needs.

And despite the fact that for the purpose of this book we are looking at experiences and channels in isolation, in reality they are interrelated, and there is a lot of cross-over. A brand like Bynd Artisan, the case for Shop Experience, is also a Bespoke Experience. The Audi Design Challenge (our case for an Event Experience) happened online, in public relations, outdoor posters and books as well as at the event space.

This book wants to be an inspiration for brands, to understand some of the most prevalent global trends in experiences. It also looks at how to use them for your own business, often with just a bit of thinking and little effort. For every trend I show, there is a case study of a brand that does this experience particularly well; I let the brand explain how they do it. This is followed by a short how-to list to help you explore that field. This is because at some companies, despite having the brand and the means, the physical spaces and the budgets, their marketers still like to work like it's 1999 and the internet never happened.

In the end, everybody wins: brands become more relevant, consumers find the experiences they are looking for, and ideally our world becomes a tiny bit more interesting, more caring and more sustainable.

CHAPTER 1

# THE BESPOKE EXPERIENCE

> Before industrialization, everything was bespoke. Shoes were made, suits were cut. Furniture was built to fit into the space. But ever since machines started making our clothes, shoes, houses, cars, furniture and accessories, things started to become both affordable and interchangeable. Bespoke was something for the elite, since having something hand-made suddenly required deeper pockets, to pay for skills that had become rare and for the time it took to make things.

It was a small article in *Monocle* that caught my eye in 2010. A young tailor had opened a small shop in Singapore's Lau Pa Sat Market, a fellow by the name of Dylan Chong. It took me a while to find the space, then I stepped inside hesitantly and started a conversation – one that is still going on more than a decade later.

Dylan has been making all my suits and shirts since then — sometimes light linen for the tropical Singapore climate, at other times thick flannel for the harsher Korean winters. And as they say, once you go bespoke, you can't go back. Now everything that is bought off the rack, even high-end brands, doesn't feel right, just because it doesn't fit right. And in addition to a keen eye for classic style and an insistence on quality, Dylan always has an opinion. Once I needed a new outfit for a 'black and white'-themed event in Korea and I texted him, 'need a black shirt'. His reply was 'nobody needs a black shirt, unless you're Kanye West. How about dark blue?'.

A few years later, I discovered a picture of a beautiful retro leather briefcase on Instagram. I wrote to the person who had posted it — Yohei Fukuda, a shoemaker from Tokyo. I asked him to make me one just like it. When I flew from Seoul to Tokyo to pick up the case, I had my feet measured for my very first pair of bespoke shoes. Others followed, and today I enjoy the excuse to travel to Tokyo for several fittings per pair, together with some green tea and some very civilized conversation about the state of the world.

But bespoke, or if we want to look at it on a wider scale and call it individualization or personalization, doesn't have to cost an arm and a leg. In a world that has become very similar (look at the shops on high streets and airports from Hong Kong to London, Munich to Moscow), people crave more individual choices, unheard stories, and products they can really make their own. Individualization is an opportunity — from initials on

Mannequin showcases the work of Dylan & Son.

handbags to completely individual notebooks by Bynd Artisan, a new Singaporean brand we will meet in the shop experience chapter. In their outlets people can not only have their notebooks branded with their own initials or names, they can also choose the paper, the cover and the binding, making the product unique and personal.

And if your product is standardized, your service doesn't have to be: A Vietnamese cobbler I use in Singapore doesn't hand out any receipts for picking up your shoes once the new soles have been fixed. "I remember you," he says. Yes, it can be a bit scary in a world where we need paper (or online) proof for everything. But I love the experience of being recognised and using my face as the pickup "receipt".

## INTERVIEW WITH Dylan Chong, Founder, Dylan & Son

*How would you describe, in one line, what your brand stands for?*
A second-generation bespoke tailoring house focused on classic menswear.

*When and how was your brand started?*
My father Peter started Oriental Tailor back in the 1970s, operating out of a pre-war shop house along Upper Bukit Timah Road. Oriental Tailor moved a few times over the years and the last shop front was situated at Lau Pa Sat on Raffles Quay.

After graduating from Lasalle College of the Arts, I flew with Singapore Airlines as a member of its cabin crew for

Tailored pants will provide a good fit and is part of the Bespoke Experience.

three years. This was so that I could save up enough capital to eventually create my own brand.

In 2010, I left the airline and took over my father's existing shopfront. I gave the tiny 90-square-foot space a complete renovation and facelift, and established a new company named Dylan & Son.

The name was chosen as a representation of two key elements – "Dylan" being my name, representing my own brand and direction, while "& Son" pays homage to the traditional way tailors name their family business, and it also represents me as being a son to my parents, trying to carry on the legacy.

Oriental Tailor became defunct and my father served as my cutter and technical advisor. I focused on branding, marketing and attended to all the customer appointments.

*When your brand was launched, what was the spark (as far as you know)? What were the consumer and market insights?*

While I was in Lasalle, I knew that I would eventually start my own label. If I were to work for somebody or a company, it would only be temporary. Having graduated with a Diploma in Fashion Design, my approach and mindset were very much set in the fashion-related realm. The idealistic plan was to start my own fashion label selling ready-to-wear (RTW) menswear. The realist side of me knew that it would be almost impossible to do that, because you need to have a huge capital to finance the branding and marketing, rental for a shopfront in a prominent address, keeping inventory, etc. Tailoring, on the other hand, requires much less capital since we only purchase materials and pay the workers once an order comes in. That was the main reason I went the tailoring route in the very beginning. Looking back, it is a good thing that I insisted on paying out of my own pocket for whatever I wanted to do. Because of this lack of funds, I went into tailoring instead of RTW fashion. I have zero faith in RTW fashion menswear in Singapore; it's simply too difficult to sustain, especially with mega brands like Uniqlo selling decent products at extremely low prices.

*What were some of the challenges the brand faced over time?*
The main challenge is the increasing overheads. As I attempted to raise the quality of our products, the costs increased exponentially.

During the initial years, most of the work was outsourced to third parties and freelance workers. The only overheads to speak of were the monthly salaries that my

The tuxedo jacket, an essential item for formal occasions.

dad and I drew. The rental wasn't too expensive as the space was small.

As we improved the quality, we had to hire full-time workers. To retain these workers, they need attractive remuneration. To house these workers, a much bigger shop is required and that equals higher rental. Higher- quality materials and machinery also need to be purchased. The cost of products increased by a few times over the years. This represented a shift in the target market – from mass to niche. There has been a considerable drop in order quantity, which affects overall sales. More marketing needs to be done and this costs money too.

The second challenge is that the number of competitors exploded in the last five years. When we started in 2010, there were fewer than five "young tailors" in Singapore. Since then, over 20 similar businesses have entered the market. A lot of them shuttered after 12 months, but there's always another new player emerging. There are also many new custom menswear shops opening up overseas, and existing ones which started to conduct trunk shows all around the world. All this meant that the proverbial pie is getting smaller and smaller. Consumers now have many more options to choose from. You really need to offer something different in order to capture a market.

Another big challenge is finding the correct manpower. It is extremely hard to find skilled craftsmen in a developed nation like Singapore. Foreign manpower policies make it very hard and expensive to hire foreign workers for a small company like ours. Head-count quotas have to be met and there are all sorts of taxes, levies and insurance to pay.

*How has the brand changed over time? What prompted these changes, and were they proactive or reactive?*
We are now a completely different company from the early days when we set up. The quality of our products is many times higher than before, and the style/general direction of the company is much more matured and classic. This is also a result of my own maturation and age.

I knew from the beginning that I wanted to cater to a higher-end market. However, I also knew that it would not be possible from the very start. I had no experience, the company lacked funds and my own mindset was much younger and naïve. Eventually, after many years of continued improvement and growth, I am now starting to fulfil my vision.

I have always believed that the only way to survive in the world of tailoring is to become very good and very expensive. The mid-tier tailors are easily replaceable as their products do not have a unique selling point. From the early 60s to the 80s, they could still get by, because there was no online shopping and few ready-to-wear brands/shops. Now, there are so many RTW options available, either in shopping malls or over the internet.

One of the major changes is that I learnt to be a cutter myself. In tailoring, the most important aspect is the cut. The cutter is the one that gives a tailor shop its "house-style". It is a way of cutting that creates a unique shape that isn't easily copied or duplicated. This is a proactive move. With so many newer custom tailoring shops opening up, I did not want to be classified together with them. I needed to have something unique to us.

Discreet buckles at the side of a pair of tailored pants still ensure a good fit when there is a change in your waistline.

*What's the one brand story you have been telling over and over?*

I have always used the analogy of disappearing hawker stalls selling traditional food in Singapore. Many of these very popular hawker stalls are slowing dying out because the founder is getting old and there is no one to take over the business. It is an absolute pity that a business that puts out a great product has to shut down because of that. This is happening because the returns do not justify the investment – simply put, it is selling a product below its true value. A lot of times, when you buy a product, you are not simply paying for the physical item; you are also buying the time of the artisan. A good product will almost always sell itself. You just have to factor in the intangibles invested into creating this product when pricing it. If the consumer fails to recognise this, then he or she is not your intended market. Trying to please everybody is the fastest way to kill a business.

*Did you set out to create a bespoke experience? How did you do that?*
I didn't. It just happened naturally.

*Has the arrival of social media and the sharing of experiences in these channels impacted your brand? Are you actively moulding your brand experiences to enable social media sharing?*
Social media has been a very strong tool for a lot of businesses, ours included. Besides word-of-mouth recommendations, most of our new clients first got to know us on social media. I am willing to explore new channels, but I generally am not very enthusiastic about being overly invested in it. Tailoring is an old trade, and I want to retain some of its old-world charm. Being too 'advanced' is not necessarily a good thing.

*Where do you see your brand in ten years?*
To be honest, I am unsure. It is so hard to replace existing manpower and if I am unable to find the appropriate workers, then it will pose a significant problem. Personally, I don't want to be overly attached to my brand; grabbing on to it for dear life. I think I would be fine if I had to eventually give it up, sell it away or just end it – if it comes down to that. I am also interested in taking on a creative-directorship role at another company at some point. It has always intrigued me: what will I do or how will I fare at another company?

# THE BESPOKE EXPERIENCE   27

If the opportunity presents itself, everyone should seize the chance to have a Bespoke Experience.

- **How to create a Bespoke Experience**
  - Start with a simple step: Give customers the chance to add their names or initials to the finished product. This is probably something you can do in the shop.
  - Then look at the choices you are offering in your manufacturing process: Are there more materials, colours or styles that you can easily add?
  - How can you personalize your service?
  - Try calling returning customers by name and even giving them small handwritten notes of thanks.

CHAPTER 2

# THE SOCIAL EXPERIENCE

> "Client needed," said my post on Facebook when I was looking for a brand to develop a campaign for with my SMU Advertising students. Immediately I received about 50 suggestions from brand owners, ranging from MNCs to SMEs, Start-Ups to established businesses. What was remarkable about this group of brands looking for free ideas was that about 50% came from the 'social enterprise' segment, many of them small businesses that wanted to do good.

I had to remember the Bill Bernbach quote that I learnt many years ago when working for DDB in China: "All of us who professionally use the mass media are the shapers of society. We can vulgarize that society. We can brutalize it. Or we can help lift it onto a higher level."

In the 60s, admen needed reminding that there was a responsibility in advertising. Clients had no qualms about pushing tobacco, alcohol or firearms, as long as the profit margin was positive.

This has changed. Today's consumers, led by millennials, are asking brands what they stand for, what their values are (often in addition to how they are being manufactured and the impact on the environment and the people who make them). More than just a hygiene factor, brand values, standing for something, can be good for business, as the Nike campaign with Colin Kaepernick has shown. It helped position the brand and actually improved Nike's bottom line, sending the share price to an all-time high and increasing online sales by 31%.

So when going through the brands that had expressed an interest to work with my students, I had a closer look at NVPC, Singapore's National Volunteer and Philanthropy Centre, where an old church friend was looking after marketing.

NVPC faced an interesting challenge – maybe it was unique to Singapore. It wasn't that there was no support for young 'ground-ups', not-for-profit startups that supported the marginalised and disenfranchised. There were quite a few government grants available, but they came from different ministries and statutory boards and were often hard to find on the various websites. In addition, what young founders often need is not just funding but know-how and mentoring.

NVPC was out to change that, and to be that one-stop-shop supporting ground-ups.

**Interview with Weina Leong, Digital Marketing and Michele Wooi, Asst Director, Strategic Partnerships, NVPC.**

*How would you describe, in one line, what your brand stands for?*
NVPC Brand: Building Singapore's City of Good Vision, a shared future where individuals, organisations and leaders come together to give their best for others.

Groundup Brand: Your idea can make a difference to others.

*What was the idea behind the Groundup campaign?*
The Groundup campaign had a two-fold objective, to spread awareness and inspiration to start groundup initiatives, and to generate leads for the non-profit incubator programme we were running, called Sandbox. This was done by sharing stories and case studies of successful groundup founders.

The target audience are those who are passionate about causes and are interested to start something. The call to action: sign up for our mailing list to receive resources to start or sustain your groundup.

*When your campaign was launched, what was the spark (as far as you know)? What were the consumer and market insights?*
Many are familiar with the charities in Singapore, but not so many are aware of the various groundup groups who also contribute to making a difference in our communities.

Consumer insights post campaign: People who saw the ads were inspired (there were many shares). Certain causes performed better on certain platforms. For example, the Groundup group doing animal therapy did exceptionally well on Instagram compared to Facebook (95% of leads came from Instagram). This finding is consistent with another NVPC product where the best performing ad on Instagram was the one featuring animals as a cause.

*What were some of the challenges you faced?*
There were three: a very limited budget, leads are expensive and we had budget cuts midway through the programme.

*How has the campaign changed over time? What prompted these changes, and were they proactive or reactive?*
The campaign consisted of six ads over a period of six months. Each video was released in line with the thematic calendar of another NVPC product (the thematic calendar shows the monthly theme and causes to focus on).

Budget cuts halfway through the campaign changed the ad strategy and content. Instead of using video content, we switched to using images.

*What's the one story you have been telling over and over?*
You can make a difference if you start something.

*Did you set out to create an experience in the field of social campaigning? How did you do that?*
All videos were posted organically on social media. All

THE SOCIAL EXPERIENCE  **33**

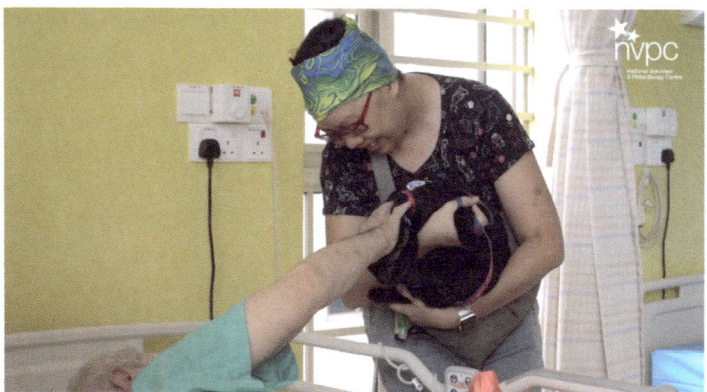

Love Kuching Project, one of the Groundup campaigns by the NVPC.

ad spend was on digital platforms such as social media (Facebook and Instagram). Besides the main objective (lead generation), we also tracked other social metrics such as reach, reactions, shares etc.

*Has the arrival of social media and the sharing of experiences in these channels impacted your brand? Are you actively moulding your brand experiences to enable social media sharing?*

Our brand is very new and has only been around for approximately a year plus, so it is difficult to ascertain. However, social media has helped us reach our target audience (youths, especially young working adults) as they are huge social media users.

Yes, we are actively moulding our brand to enable social media sharing. We have a Facebook closed group to engage Groundup leaders, and we are tapping on our organisation's (NVPC) Facebook page to run paid ads and organic posts where relevant.

Our marketing strategy is digitally led and in line with the concept of social media sharing. We do try to tailor the content and format to the audience in social media, for example, by having videos instead of pictures.

*Where do you see the impact of your campaign in ten years?*

Groundups become more widely known, and are recognised and appreciated in society. More are stepping forward to start groundups.

THE SOCIAL EXPERIENCE    35

Light of Hope, another Groundup campaign, looks at how people view mental illness and seeks to change their perceptions.

Kodrah is for everyone, it's not just for Eurasians,

It's a very diverse community.

Kristang is one of the languages spoken by the Eurasian community and Kodrah Kristang seeks to increase its awareness beyond the community.

### How to create a Social Experience

- Think about the values your brand has, apart from being commercially viable.
- Determine how you are expressing these values.
- Align these values with the values of the target group your are pursuing.
- More than just donating a percentage of profits to charity, people like to get involved. So give your customers an active role in supporting your values.
- Make sure the chosen social causes are related to your business and they are something you genuinely care about.

CHAPTER 3

# THE EVENT EXPERIENCE

> It was a cold afternoon a few weeks after I had landed in Seoul to take up my new position as Marketing Director for Audi Korea. Slowflakes were falling outside, and we were sitting around the conference table, looking at the latest research about reasons for car purchases.

The ranking didn't surprise us. Design was still the number one reason for buying a specific car brand. "This is good," said my colleague Jun Park. "We have the best design." Maybe, but how would you measure good design, and how would Koreans know that our design is better?

"Association" was the word that came up in the discussion. What if we don't talk about car design but about design in general? What if we associated with good design in other fields like furniture?

"What if….", I started to say, and saw the excited and somewhat worried smiles in the faces of my team, "what if we gave people a platform to create design?"

This was how the Audi Design Challenge Korea was born. Once a year, we'd call on design students to submit their designs in the fields of furniture, accessories, music and motion pictures. A group of experts would select the top four ideas per segment and they would mentor the students during the actual production process. The 16 finalists would be featured in a design exhibition.

The set-up for the 2014 Audi Design Challenge.

We collaborated with *Design Today*, the leading design magazine in Korea, and reached out to the design community. We were met with enthusiasm and open arms. Professors and famous designers helped mentor students, and being a member of the judging panel was always an inspirational and humbling experience for me.

The final exhibition, hosted in different locations but eventually finding its appropriate home in Zaha Hadid's Dongdaemun Design Plaza, was a masterpiece of my event team and their agency. It was a consistent expression of the clean, form-follows-function principles of Audi design, expressed in daring and useful, visionary and impressive pieces. And it wasn't just the subject matter that made the statement of 'Audi knows design'. Everything, from the decoration of the hall, the invitations, the food and the book documenting the winners, spoke the same language and paid into the same benefit.

**Interview with Youngjun Park, Marketing Director, Audi Korea.**

*How would you describe, in one line, what your brand stands for?*
We fearlessly drive progress and shape the future of individual mobility. It means we do not just build cars, we unleash the beauty of mobility. For us, this is *Vorsprung durch Technik* (German phrase translated as progress through technology).

Exhibition showcase of the entries for the design competition.

*When and how was your brand started?*
Audi was established in 1909 by August Horch. The Audi four-ring emblem symbolizes the merger in 1932 of four previously independent motor-vehicle manufacturers: Audi, DKW, Horch and Wanderer. In 1969 Auto Union GmbH amalgamated with NSU Motorenwerke AG.

*When your brand was launched, what was the spark (as far as you know)? What were the consumer and market insights?*
We differentiate ourselves from our competitors by challenging ourselves to innovate our brand and products. Here are some of the firsts that Audi achieved.
1921: Left-hand drive
1923: Wind tunnel test
1933: Front-wheel driving
1937: Record to reached top speed of 400km
1938: Side test
1980: 4-wheel driving 'quattro' in a sedan
1989: Turbo direct diesel engine TDI
1993: Developed the aluminum body 'ASF'
2006: Wins Le Mans 24-hour race with R10 TDI
2009: Designs a 100% electronic sport car 'Audi e-tron'
2012: Win Le Mans 24-hour race with hybrid 'Audi R18 e-tron quattro'

*What were some of the challenges the brand faced over time?*
The greatest challenge is that Audi has to forecast the future to meet customer expectations. The brand only

can lead the market when the brand meets the customer's expectation such as design, performance, value and brand image.

*How has the brand changed over time? What prompted these changes, and were they proactive or reactive?*
Audi has changed as we are much more progressive in design. Audi has many advanced technologies but those are rational and in fact factors to push you to buy. The design of the car itself is the most instinctive factor to define the brand. After changing the design, Audi became a desirable brand to get. The iconic design "touches" the customers' heart and it remains in their mind longer.

*What's the one brand story you have been telling over and over?*
Definitely it's brand awareness around the world. Audi never stops in brand promotion and marketing. In this case, we wanted to build and increase Audi's association with design. Rather than directly talking about the design of the car, we thought it would be good to co-create content together with young designers from Korean universities. The students were asked to design objects in the four categories of accessories, furniture, music and moving image. A jury of established designers shortlisted the finalists and the students worked with mentors from their field to actually produce the objects they designed. The 16 finalists were then the highlight of a carefully curated exhibition in Zaha Hadid's Dongdaemun Design Plaza in Seoul. We invited our VIPs, customers and the public to

attend the event to learn more about Audi design. We also incorporated some cars in the display; it was where visitors could listen to the four selected music pieces.

*Did you set out to create an experience in the field of events? How did you do that?*
Experience Marketing is the most emotional marketing activity. People can see, feel, experience and touch the brand through the events. It has to deliver the message and "touch" people's mind to be unforgettable. That means we have to provide an event that money cannot buy. Everything works together – sights, sounds, smell and taste, through the food we offer.

*Tell us a bit about the Audi Design Challenge, how it worked and most importantly the event and exhibition.*
Audi has always been one step ahead of its competitors, setting a new standard with its innovative technology and design under the corporate slogan of Vorsprung durch Technik. The Audi Design Challenge has been the talk of the town with its exhibition of highly sophisticated pieces of artwork. Many talented young designers are given the opportunity to present their work.

*Does your brand cater to the sharing economy? Or do you take the opposite route?*
While we offer some mobility options that include sharing or co-owning options for cars, our target group is still very much into selecting their perfect car, individualising it and then using it for themselves and their family.

# LOUNGE STOOL
Comfortable and multi-functional lounge stool for AUDI

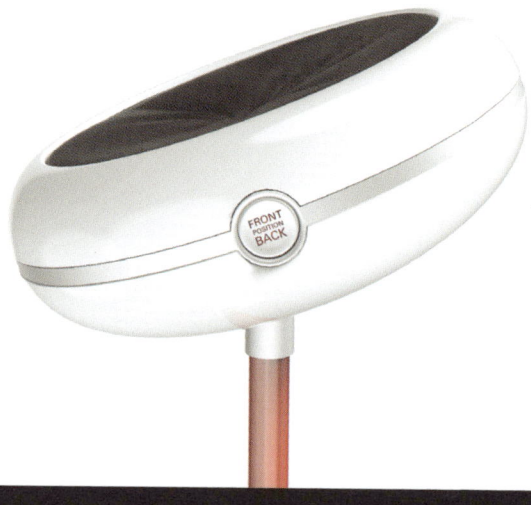

Submissions from the Audi Design Challenge.

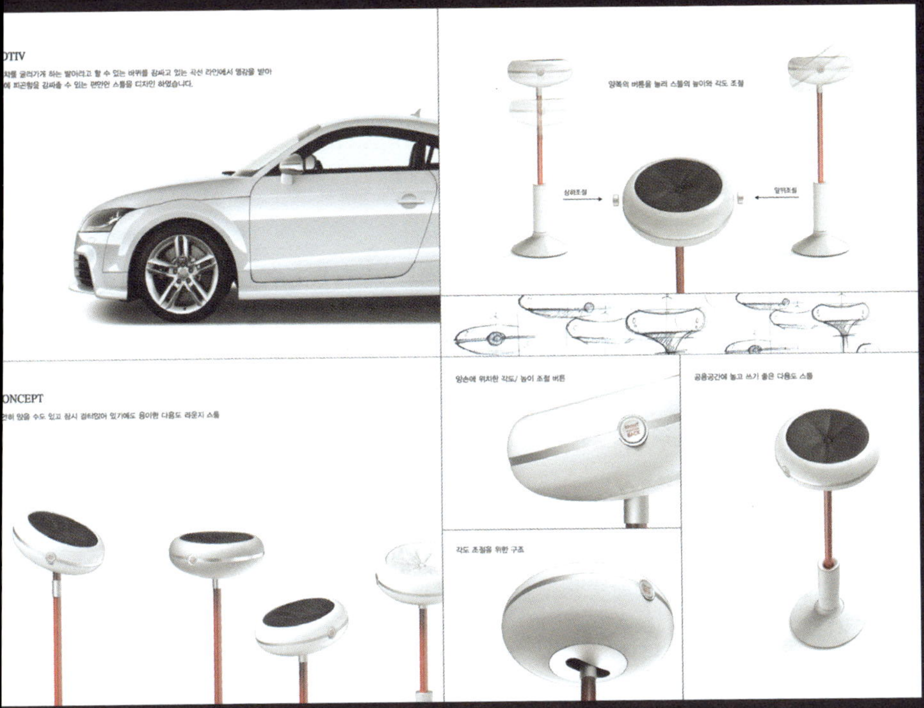

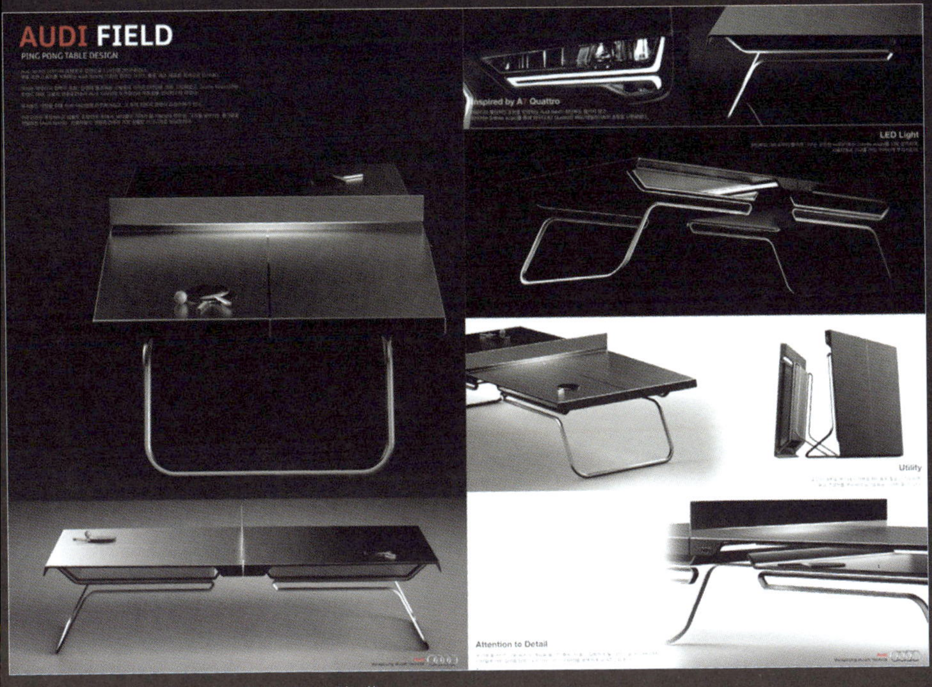

# AUDI FIELD
PING PONG TABLE DESIGN

Submissions from the Audi Design Challenge.

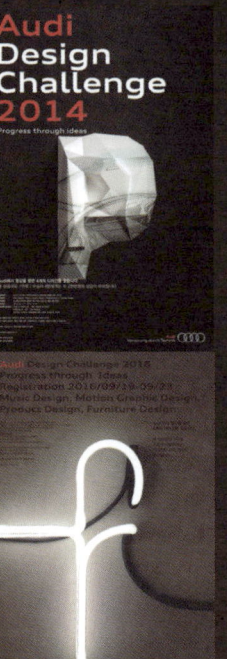

Submissions from the Audi Design Challenge.

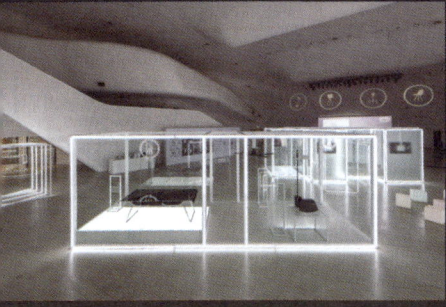

Exhibition showcasing the Audi Design Challenge.

*Has the arrival of social media and the sharing of experiences in these channels impacted your brand? Are you actively moulding your brand experiences to enable social media sharing?*

Social media is the most important marketing tool these days. One of the most important success factors for SNS (social networking service) is what do we want to communicate and who do we want to communicate with. If I compare PPL (pay per lead) and SNS, the purpose of brand awareness might be the same but SNS fits more naturally into people's daily life.

We don't have to set up the brand image, we just integrate the brand into people's lifestyle and consumers will be looking for it. We are working closely with Choi Siwon from the K-pop group Super Junior who is our brand ambassador. We encourage him to post about the car that he drives and the Audi events that he attends, thereby reaching his millions of followers on social media

Participants and the judges for the 2015 Audi Design Challenge.

that normally we couldn't reach. And naturally we are also using our own channels in Korea like Facebook and Instagram.

*Where do you see your brand in ten years?*
I'm sure Audi will see advances in terms of design, mobility, AI, electronics, and even lifestyle. Audi is not only a car, Audi provides mobility.

● **How to create an Event Experience**
- Think about a topic that is close to your brand so you can own it.
- Brand the event as yours; being a sponsor amongst many is wasted money.
- Look at the event as a holistic experience and make sure that everything visitors see, feel, smell or hear is consistent.
- Invite the right people and keep it exclusive.
- Use online media to share the event with a wider audience.

CHAPTER 4

# THE BRICK-AND-MORTAR SHOP EXPERIENCE

> Digital has taken over the shopping experience in many fields, and the likes of Amazon and Shopee make the buying of brands convenient and often cheaper. Comparison is easy, and we can lean on customer reviews to decide if the intended product is right for us. Does that mean shops are dead?

Selling via digital platforms doesn't work for every product. Luxury products want to be experienced, touched and tried, cars need to be driven, clothes tried on (never mind bespoke, which pretty much relies on personal interaction and measurement). And some people miss the actual personal interaction during the shopping experience, the conversation with a knowledgeable sales person, the glass of

The Bynd Artisan atelier at ION Orchard.

champagne in the high-end boutique, the easy browsing of shelves.

For centuries, brands have thought about ways of making the brick-and-mortar experience more interesting or just different. The glass of champagne plays a part, but so does the look and feel and smell of the shop. Shanghai Tang was amongst the first to develop a signature scent, known as "Ginger Flower", for their shops, and Abercrombie and Fitch created a whole new experience – the shop as a club – complete with dim lighting, loud music and their own signature scent.

As the competition increases, not just from digital platforms, brands are now thinking of offering an unusual but also educational shopping experience. Bynd Artisan, a young Singaporean brand, is one of the leaders in this field. In its shops customers can select their own choice of paper, cover materials and binding for notebooks and diaries (a good example of a bespoke experience). They can also watch the artisans in the shop putting it all together and applying names or initials. This makes it both an Instagram-worthy event and also makes people spend more time in the shop and leave with something truly unique.

If your brand already has a brick-and-mortar presence, think about how you can make it more interesting. Years ago, during a brief for my students on a communication project for Page One, the bookstore, Kelley Cheng said about ideas for shop windows which were part of the brief: "Don't think books. Think fashion." Or car brands – they already have those huge, expensive showrooms that many people find cold and somewhat intimidating. What an opportunity to re-invent this space and use it not just for the display of cars but for a 360° experience from materials to the fun of driving via virtual reality (VR)!

Some are already doing this: my students recently presented the Decathlon sports brand. In their "lab" shops they are creating surfaces to test running shoes and even a hiking path with gravel. Consumers can test-ride the bicycles and experience the brand hands-on.

Japan's Marui department store takes the in-store experience one step further. In its space shoppers can have their measurements taken, test digital equipment or trade anime collectibles – but there is no pressure to buy.

The *Nikkei Asian Review* describes the experience as follows: "At some of its department stores in prime locations, perhaps those near a major train station, Marui is leasing floor space to internet companies so web shoppers can try on or get a feel for something that caught their fancy online."

One day in late August at Shibuya Modi, a sales assistant at a made-to-order suit shop was helping a male visitor. "You don't need to buy here, sir," the salesperson said. "Please take your time to consider."

This picks up on a behaviour that consumers are already showing: checking out the merchandise in physical stores, then completing the purchase online.

## Interview with James Quan & Winnie Chan, Founders, Bynd Artisan

*How would you describe, in one line, what your brand stands for?*
It is difficult to express what Bynd Artisan stands for in one line but we believe therein lies the beauty of the brand we have built. It is multi-faceted, has a soul and communicates the vision and ideals that we want to stand for in a sentimental way.

In four sentences, this is what we do. Born from a rich heritage of craftsmanship, Bynd Artisan offers customised and personalised leather and paper gifts for everyone, for any occasion. Bynd Artisan encourages its audience to immerse themselves in the process of creating the perfect gift and offers workshops to share the joy of craft. The brand also provides a platform for talents and creatives to

James Quan and Winnie Chan, founders of Bynd Artisan.

celebrate innovation and design through collaborations. This passion for design extends to corporate gifting with bespoke creations and custom personalisation, enabling clients to share the perfect gift from the heart.

In four points, this is what we stand for:

**Business Innovation.** Rekindling of traditional craftsmanship in a digital age through job redesign.

**Design Thinking.** Placing emphasis on the return on experience. Celebrating the spirit of artisanal excellence through customer engagement in storytelling and sincere customer service. We are committed in creating positive and meaningful interactions with our audiences.

**Respect.** Paying tribute to our craftsmen who have spent their whole lifetimes honing their craft, mindful of using environmentally friendly and sustainable materials.

**Changemaker.** Nurturing entrepreneurship, championing equality and diversity, and promoting passion in the arts and design. We hope to inspire those who feel trapped in traditional sunset industries, those who feel they are too old to go into a new field having invested years in their current career, and to encourage active aging.

*When and how was your brand started?*
Bynd Artisan was founded in 2014, as a modern interpretation of Winnie's traditional family bookbinding business. In the 1940s, Winnie's grandfather founded the Goy Liang Book-Making Company, the first bookbindery

One of the orginal Heidelberg printing presses used by the company.

in Singapore. Drawing from this rich heritage, we sought to revitalise the bookbinding industry and reach out to the younger generations amidst this digital age, whilst preserving the artisanal spirit.

Born from a strong legacy of makers in traditional bookmaking and leather craftsmanship, the brand melds 100 years of shared experience from its band of veteran craftsmen who have spent their lives seeking to hone their skills to perfection.

The traditional method of bookbinding is done by hand.

*When your brand was launched, what was the spark (as far as you know)? What were the consumer and market insights?*

The driving force behind the inception of Bynd Artisan was a strong passion for well-made paper and leather goods, combined with a need to survive and thrive in a seemingly sunset industry. At the time, the traditional bookbinding industry was largely made of mass-produced stationery, catering to students and offices; this itself was under threat from increasing digitalisation. To stay relevant and thrive, we were aware of the need to revitalise the industry and cater to new audiences with innovative products.

By creating lifestyle products and offering customisation and personalisation options, we added the element of uniqueness into our products and made paper products chic and sexy. Our range of products also cater to a wide variety of consumers. In the beginning our target audience were the young working adults, but over time we noticed that our customers range from teenagers to mature customers.

*What were some of the challenges the brand faced over time?*

One of the hurdles we faced in the early days was trying to gain traction in the retail scene and for consumers to get to know of the brand. Initially, it was difficult to find malls or retail spaces which would feature paper and leather stationery, as most were uncertain about whether a small homegrown brand would be well-received. The turning point occurred when a prominent department store along Orchard Road invited Bynd Artisan to set up a shop-in-shop.

Another early challenge was for the senior staff, previously from the production floor, to adapt to the retail environment. The senior staff were initially apprehensive about working in the frontline and interacting with customers daily. This was overcome by conducting training sessions to upskill them and encouraging them constantly, adding on to what we envisioned in small steps. It was not long before our senior staff saw the respect and felt the love from our customers and went on to embrace their new roles as brand ambassadors.

*How has the brand changed over time? What prompted these changes, and were they proactive or reactive?*
Recognizing the importance of e-commerce, Bynd Artisan has a webstore on our site that allows customers to customise and/or personalize our products. The webstore gives consumers added convenience to browse and shop our products online and allows the brand to reach overseas customers. The offline/online concept was something we had hoped to achieve from the beginning.

To stay relevant, Bynd Artisan continuously innovates in product design to offer the best in stationery and leather goods. As part of this, we work with homegrown talents across various industries to create exclusive products and capsule collections. In the process, Bynd Artisan seeks to enhance the vibrancy of the local design scene and promote collaboration amongst local creatives. This principle of collaborative innovation has

Workshop for participants to add a personal touch to their items at the Holland Village atelier.

been implemented proactively since the early days of the company.

*What's the one brand story you have been telling over and over?*
One story which we tell often is that of our Master Craftsman Mr Chong Beng Cheng, who has over five decades of experience. Mr Chong started out working in Winnie's family business, and later joined Bynd Artisan

The Bynd Artisan atelier at Raffles City.

as our Master Craftsman. He is an example of how the brand's senior staff have upskilled and adapted to the changing times of the industry. From a stern and quiet man who mostly kept to himself, Mr Chong has become the brand's iconic poster boy, learned to relax and even crack jokes to engage workshop participants. We daresay that Mr Chong (at 77 years old this year) has finally found his purpose in life (sharing his knowledge and experience in craft) and truly enjoys his work knowing what he stands for – a healthy active ager still contributing to society.

*Did you set out to create an experience in the field of bespoke/shop experience? How did you do that?*
A holistic retail experience has always been at the core of Bynd Artisan. One of the key goals when launching Bynd Artisan was to create an experiential retail concept that collaborates with artistic talents, personalises paper and leather accessories, and runs crafting workshops. As part of this, we involve consumers in the process of handcrafting gifts or items for their own use. This model has proven to be successful, as Bynd Artisan was awarded Best Shopping Experience at the 2017 Singapore Tourism Awards.

To curate such an immersive experience, our ateliers feature a craftsman's station where customers can watch 'live' as their items are being made or personalised. We also offer workshops at a few ateliers, encouraging customers to be "hands-on" and learn a crafting skill from our craftsmen.

Each atelier also incorporates a sense of tradition and embraces the company's rich heritage through its décor, which includes vintage machinery and memorabilia from Winnie's family business. Along with carefully planned and decorated store interiors, these references to the brand's heritage and craftsmanship come together to create an all-round shopping experience.

Mr Chong Beng Cheng (*above and opposite*) has worked for the company for over five decades. It was then known as Goy Liang Book-Making Company. Today, he is Bynd Artisan's Master Craftsman and is an example of how the brand's senior staff have upskilled and adapted to the times.

*Has the arrival of social media and the sharing of experiences in these channels impacted your brand? Are you actively moulding your brand experiences to enable social media sharing?*

Recognizing the importance of social media in creating and reaching a large audience, Bynd Artisan makes efforts to curate the shopping experience to encourage social media sharing, from the décor to the ambience to our products. Even our senior craftsmen are exposed to social media. They encourage customers to share their shopping experience on social media, and even make use of the platform to interact with consumers.

Social media also plays a large part in our marketing. We harness various social media platforms such as Instagram and Facebook, which we use for advertising, brand engagement and to interact with consumers. In keeping up with the times, Bynd Artisan also makes use of new features on social media such as the Instagram Shop function to create an engaging experience online as well.

*Where do you see your brand in ten years?*

In ten years, we envision Bynd Artisan to have expanded across the region and beyond, with ateliers overseas and an expanded e-commerce presence. So far, Bynd Artisan has spread awareness through East and Southeast Asia, with pop-up stores in Hong Kong, Shanghai and Manila.

Bynd Artisan also has a corporate bespoke arm, which caters to a broad variety of clientele, including SMEs, private banks, government ministries and MNCs. In the coming years, we seek to expand our presence in the corporate gifting sector and overseas markets.

### How to create a Shop Experience
- Think about what you can do, such as appealing to the senses, that can't be done online.
- Break the segment convention. Who says shops have to look and feel like all other shops?
- Start thinking from your brand. What makes it different and how can you help people experience the difference in your shop?
- Use the space for more than display – make it social or educational.
- Make the human interaction that can only happen in a shop special and memorable through training and special touches.

CHAPTER 5

# THE HERITAGE EXPERIENCE

> Having a long history and a story to tell is a good thing. Consumers like a brand that has been around for decades or even centuries as it is seen as more trustworthy and reliable. There is something reassuring in knowing that your grandfather has used the same brand before you.

The trap, of course, is to become too traditional, backward-looking instead of forward. That's why I try to avoid the word "traditional" in branding projects and instead use "legacy". This has a similar meaning but is much more forward-looking.

Many established brands have struggled to learn from the past, their history and achievements, and use them to re-invent the brand as a modern brand with a legacy. Burberry is a good example of a brand that managed to modernize without leaving the past behind. Another one is Eu Yan Sang.

Eu Yan Sang is a Singaporean brand with a long, interesting history that has gone international. Richard Eu and his team have managed to keep the good of the past, and all the benefits of Traditional Chinese Medicine (TCM), and take it into the present and future, creating a brand experience that feels modern and clean. TCM for the 21st century.

### Interview with Richard Eu, Non-Executive Chairman, Eu Yan Sang

*How would you describe, in one line, what your brand stands for?*
Eu Yan Sang is your trusted health partner known for its quality and deep insight in TCM.

*When and how was your brand started?*
Eu Yan Sang was founded by my great-grandfather Eu Kong in 1879 as a means of offering health solutions to tin mine workers.

*When your brand was launched, what was the spark (as far as you know)? What were the consumer and market insights?*
Back in 1879, when my great grandfather started the business in Gopeng – where Chinese sojourners were attracted to economic opportunities in tin-mining – the

Richard Eu, non-executive chairman, Eu Yan Sang.

Eu Yan Sang's original store.

living conditions at the tin mines were very poor, and the workers had no access to health care. A lot of them turned to opium as a form of pain relief.

My great-grandfather converted an opium den into a provision shop, and offered Chinese medicines to address the societal and health needs at that time.

*What were some of the challenges the brand faced over time?*
The biggest challenge for our brand is staying relevant to our target audience. As our society and economy have progressed, what was relevant 140 years ago is no longer relevant today.

From our product offering to product packaging, product communication and distribution channel, we have to constantly innovate ourselves to be relevant to the health needs of different demographics and different lifestyles.

*How has the brand changed over time? What prompted these changes, and were they proactive or reactive?*
The brand had to be updated to be relevant to modern consumer needs. If this didn't happen, there would be no more consumers left. There was a combination of proactive and reactive changes made along our transformation journey.

We have been one of the early adopters of science in our industry since the 1990s. When there was increasing awareness and demand for evidence-based and safety-assured health solutions, if our brand did not change to embrace science and technology in the provision of products and services, we would not be relevant to our consumers.

When mass-built public housing was introduced in Singapore, if we stayed put in the city and did not expand our retail footprint into residential areas, we would not be our consumers' choice of everyday health partner today.

*What's the one brand story you have been telling over and over?*
Our products have been able to help consumers in their health needs, like a chronic cough, pain relief or some other medical conditions. I find real-life cases most convincing, and I would share them over and over again to help more people.

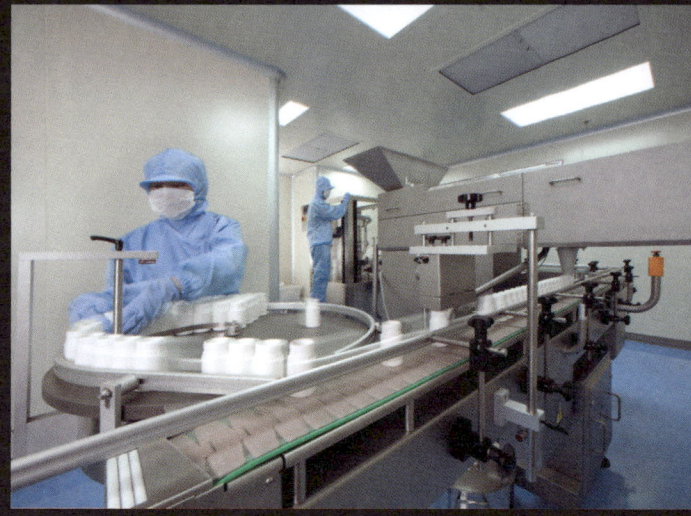

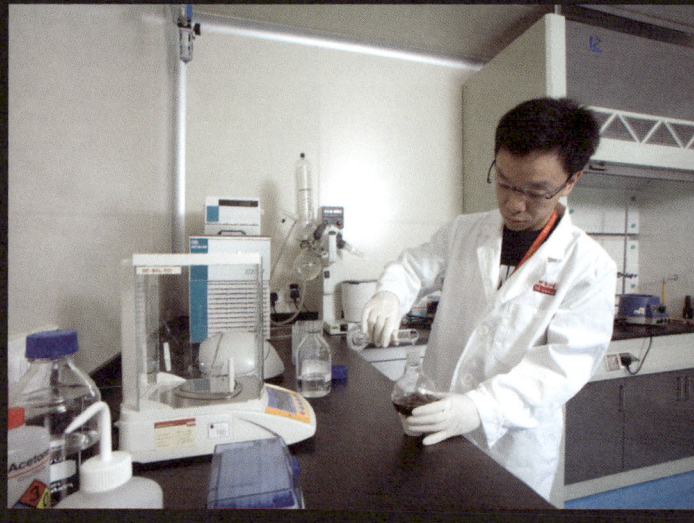

*This page*:
Eu Yan Sang incorporates the latest technology and has strict quality control in the manufacture of its TCM products.

*Opposite*:
All the company's shops and TCM clinics have been designed to reflect a modern style that appeals to both the young and old.

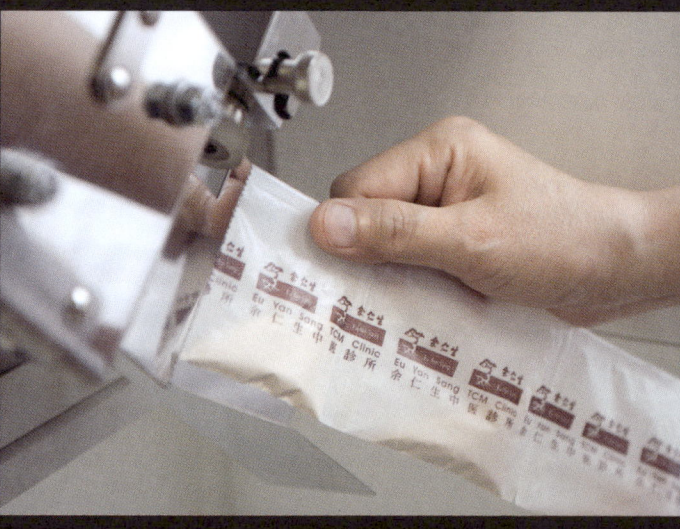

Eu Yan Sang's original signboard.

*Did you set out to create an experience in the field of medical/heritage? How did you do that? And how do you combine TCM with modern medicine?*

We have come a long way, offering health solutions backed by a deep wisdom and insights in TCM. We gained trust from people through their positive experience with our products and services. Most importantly, our products and treatments have to work for our consumers, then only will it be passed down from generation to generation.

 We do not combine TCM with modern medicine, but we seek to validate TCM with modern science. We seek to modernise TCM by developing more solutions that are more relevant to modern lifestyle needs.

 We do not ditch old practices entirely to look modern. Over time, we learned to separate the wheat from the chaff in TCM, and we seek to reinterpret this ancient wisdom in a way we can connect with today's consumers.

*Has the arrival of social media and the sharing of experiences in these channels impacted your brand? Are you actively moulding your brand experiences to enable social media sharing?*
Yes, social media enables us to tell our story and help us spread through word-of-mouth in a more effective manner. We have an active presence on social media and have been trying to get our users to be more forthcoming in sharing their experiences.

*Where do you see your brand in ten years?*
TCM has a huge role in health and wellness and it can benefit more people. I hope to see the Eu Yan Sang brand and products transcend borders and cultures in 10 year's time.

### How to create a Heritage Experience
- Look at your brand's history and tell the story – online and offline – in your shops, your packaging and your products.
- Be proud of having a history.
- Don't confuse having a heritage with being traditional or old-fashioned. Your content can look back; your look and feel must be current.
- Understand what it was that gave your brand longevity and use it today.
- Hire young marketers and creatives, educate them about your brand, and be open to their fresh ideas.

CHAPTER 6

# THE CULTURAL EXPERIENCE

> In a world that is becoming increasingly similar, people want to experience something unique and different – something that is worth a story or sharing about. Travel used to be a good way to pick up new experiences, but it wasn't easy to find genuine local experiences for single travellers. The internet is full of rip-offs, where locals (and who can blame them) are out to make a quick buck by commercializing culture.

The alternative, going on a package tour, took some of the headache out of planning, but moving in a big group isn't everybody's cup of tea. The experiences offered are also often money-driven, like visiting "factories" where carpets or local crafts are made, with the convenient opportunity (and often a lot of pressure) to buy such handicrafts in the adjacent shop.

A Chinese calligraphy experience in Shanghai.

Airbnb changed all that. Suddenly it was possible to stay in people's homes within residential neighbourhoods. To 'live like the locals', complete with food shopping, cooking and meeting the neighbours. Airbnb quickly realised that travellers wanted more than chance encounters with the local culture, now that they were staying in the midst of it. The company offered Airbnb Experiences, curated workshops and tours at the location of the booking. Recently, they went even more extreme and launched Airbnb Adventures. These are tours that go into the depths of local culture and wildlife, with transport, food and accommodation provided. "All you have to do is show up," as they say.

But what if you wanted to experience local culture right where you lived? Because your grandmother told you about it but you never lived through it yourself? Or because you'd like to see (and try) a dying art before it disappears? This is where Culturally comes in. Starting in Singapore and Shanghai, the team has created local cultural experiences that are real, hands-on, and often run by family-owned businesses in the nth generation.

   The Culturally vision is to build a worldwide community where people understand different cultures. Their mission statement is that Culturally strives to foster inclusive communities and preserve heritage by providing access to global cultural experiences that are hands-on and traditional.

### Interview with Lee Jacin, Cofounder of Culturally

*How would you describe, in one line, what your brand stands for?*
Building human connections. We believe in inclusion and preservation. Our vision is to build a worldwide community where people form human connections through understanding different cultures.

   Through Culturally, we hope to connect people through authentic cultural experiences, and at the same time, preserve heritage for future generations.

*When and how was your brand started?*
Culturally was born out of a curiosity to understand other cultures, and a passion to bridge cultures all over the world.

   In 2016, on a solo trip to South Korea, I wanted to try *samulnori* (traditional Korean percussion) with a local ensemble. It took me hours browsing sites on YouTube, Instagram, Facebook, Googl,e etc before I finally found a *samulnori* drummer *on* LinkedIn (through a YouTube caption). She was kind enough to invite me to attend a group rehearsal she had organized the next day. Other ensemble members who made up this *salmunori* group were musicians from all over the world who had somehow made their homes in Seoul and banded together over this common love for *salmunori* to create beautiful music. This essence of inclusion and joy found in a shared passion sparked the motivation in me to want to create a platform where more people could find like-minded individuals and build on their passions together. This was where the idea for a platform that would aid in building communities through shared cultural experiences began.

As my cofounder Michael and I started exploring this idea and conducting market research, we looked back on our respective personal backgrounds and areas of competitive advantage and decided on Shanghai as our launch pad for the following reasons.

For me, I grew up moving around every three to four years: from Singapore, to Taiwan, Hong Kong, Beijing, Shanghai and New York City, I experienced firsthand how expatriates in all these cities tended to live in a bubble, not of their own volition, but purely by virtue of there not being a central medium connecting locals and foreigners. As a child and teenager, I had spent 10 years in China, but I made more American, British and Korean friends from the international schools I had attended than local Chinese friends.

School was the medium for me to be introduced to all these global cultures, but local citizens (Chinese in this case) were not allowed in international schools, so I had no way to interact with Chinese (local) culture. I thought Shanghai would be the perfect place to kickstart Culturally because already I knew who our clients were going to be. International schools, universities and corporate MNCs who wanted their students/community to learn about Chinese (local) culture, but didn't know where to begin. Tourists, expatriates, and even local Chinese who wanted to know more about Chinese heritage and global culture but didn't know where to start. Thus, in 2017, our brand was launched.

According to co-founder Michael: "I had similar reasons for starting Culturally. The reasons are linked to my background. I spent the good part of 25 years in Australia before moving to Shanghai. Because I am of Chinese heritage and I speak Mandarin, it was a great experience for me to be able to live in the thick of it all. I was able to understand various aspects of life as a local resident in China as well as life as a local resident in a Western country. This dual perspective provided me with a very different experience in China. The biggest observation that I made was that many foreign tourists or expats who visited China were not able to appreciate Chinese culture the same way as I did. I always thought it was a shame to not have that complete picture. I do believe that the value that an individual gets from understanding the local culture with great depth will enhance their time in a foreign place. Many moments that foreign visitors have when visiting China would become 'interesting' and make sense. I wanted Culturally's brand to represent the reason for someone's improved cultural empathy and understanding."

Participants at a corporate family day event learn all about batik painting.

Pamphlets are given out at events to introduce other cultural experiences organised by the company.

*When your brand was launched, what was the spark (as far as you know)?*
I would say the spark was that *salmunori* experience for me in Korea. Just being able to enjoy such a wonderful cultural experience I was interested in with other like-minded individuals made me feel: "I must not be the only one who wants more of this, who wants exactly this."

People crave human connection over shared interests. Real human connections are formed when a group of people come together and explore or build upon a passion through no other motive than pure enjoyment. We strove to find truly passionate people who were experts in their field or art. They must also want to share what they know because they see the value in preserving heritage, and globalizing it so that a wider audience can enjoy it.

*When your brand was launched, what were the consumer and market insights?*
Prior to launching the brand, we conducted a few market surveys and the facts were thus: 59% were interested in cooking experiences, 49% were interested in traditional or artisanal workshops, and 22% were interested in musical experiences. There was a high 79% of consumers who professed an interest in cultural experiences; of that percentage, 36% had never participated in one because they either didn't know such experiences existed for participation or they didn't know where to find such experiences.

Today, every travel report out there illustrates an increase in experiential travel. Tourists are no longer just interested in jumping on a city tour bus on a day-trip around town or taking photos of iconic tourist attractions. Of course, a lot of people still enjoy sights, but the implied utility derived from other experiences whilst visiting a city on short-term holidays or longer-term stays has greatly increased.

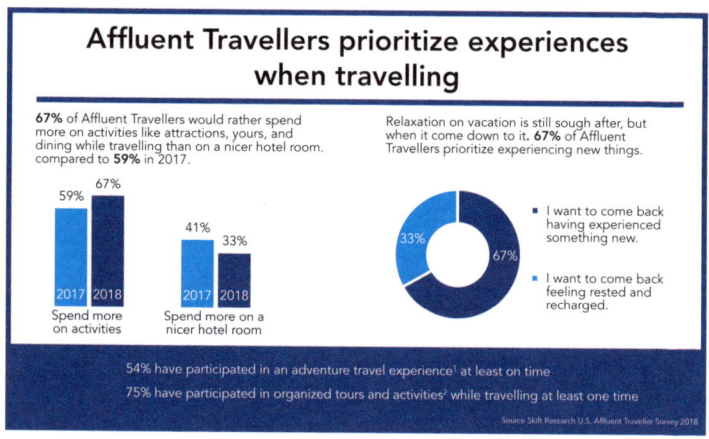

Research figures showing that travellers prioritize experiences when travelling. Source: Skift Research U.S. Affluent Traveller Trends 2018.

From a macro-perspective, according to research analysts at investment bank SunTrust Robinson Humphrey, a key market insight has been cited as an addressable market of US$160 to US$180 billion and growing for the global tours and activities segment. Additionally, a 2018 Skift Research survey indicated that 67% of affluent travellers would rather spend their money on activities than on a nicer hotel, up eight percentage points from the previous year (2017). Given the above data, we were confident that our brand could prevail in this market. And so far, it's proven so!

*What were some of the challenges the brand faced over time?*

In the beginning, because we were a new company operating a marketplace business model, our brand was unknown. There was no brand recognition to speak of, hence traditional suppliers were hesitant to join us.

A key reason for this hesitation, as we learnt over our many interactions, was the lack of understanding of how a marketplace business model works. Hence, education about a platform like ours to traditional suppliers was a vital first step in introducing our brand into the market.

Shanghai, in particular, operated in a very different way from a typical city in the Western market. Stylistically, branding and marketing differed vastly, so the type of content material we received from our vendors was often not what we knew the Western market would appreciate. Because a majority of our suppliers were traditional offline

Participants at a dim sum making experience.

A participant smiles in delight as she makes the perfect xiao long bao.

businesses, they often had no idea of the importance placed upon high-definition media content, and so we had to personally visit studios and craft content ourselves with hired photographers and videographers.

We worked hard at building our relationships with our vendors, to introduce the many benefits of working with a platform like ours, and to prove to them that we wanted what they wanted; which was to promote culture as a primary goal.

As the brand started gaining recognition in the minds of our suppliers of hands-on, cultural and heritage experiences, to further engage with our stakeholders, we recently re-branded the reference of our suppliers into "Culturally Ambassadors (CAs)".

The big challenge moving forward is of course differentiating our brand from all the other experience platforms out there. How can we achieve our goal of allowing more people to understand and empathize with

The Culturally team and Culturally Ambassadors who attended the *sashiko* stitching experience.

culture/cultural experiences without being seen as just another generic marketplace or e-commerce ticketing platform? How can we differentiate ourselves from established brands out there like Airbnb, GoVoyagin, Viator or GetYourGuide?

In the spirit of inclusion, we invite our CAs to attend other CA experiences so that they can learn from one another. We are also exploring free training sessions to provide CAs whose first language is not English to better prepare themselves when they conduct workshops in English.

*How has the brand changed over time? What prompted these changes, and were they proactive or reactive?*
I don't think our brand has changed much over time. We've stayed true to our North Star, which is to share the beauty of cultures with more and more people all over the world and bridge people through these shared experiences.

We maintain our focus on authentic experiences, taught by passionate artists, musicians and makers as well as multi-generational businesses. The importance of building human connections is never lost in us, as we practise meaningful conversations daily within our teams and with our Culturally Ambassadors.

That said, whilst the brand initially was targeted at tourists and long-term expatriates travelling into and living in a foreign country, we quickly realised that a large part of our users were local residents with an interest in experiencing cultural workshops reflecting global cultures. Reacting to this, we expanded our offerings from local experiences to global experiences. Through Culturally, #rallyers who can't afford the time or monetary expense to travel can experience global cultures in their own backyard. This is something that we feel is truly meaningful and reflects our brand's mission and values.

On another note, a proactive brand change that we initiated was renaming our vendors to Culturally Ambassadors. We wanted everyone to feel like they were part of our family, because that's what they were. Culturally isn't a platform like other platforms; we genuinely care about our Ambassadors, and they genuinely care about us.

*What's the one brand story you have been telling over and over?*
Culturally was borne out of a curiosity to understand other cultures, and a passion to bridge cultures all over the world. The word "rally" as a verb means to "(cause to)

THE CULTURAL EXPERIENCE  **93**

Students from New York University studying in Shanghai taking a Culturally Wing Chun experience.

Hands-on woodworking experience in action.

come together in order to provide support or make a shared effort" and that's what we're doing. We're calling out to people to come together to provide support in preserving heritage and understanding other cultures so that we can be one step closer to an inclusive world.

Ambitiously, we want to work towards "world peace". Hatred and division come from being different and not understanding and not learning. Whilst Culturally experiences are not meant to help you fully understand a foreign culturem, we hope to bring you closer to *wanting to understand*. By getting hands-on in a fun and engaging workshop, learning about different cultures through producing something beautiful and tangible, we hope to spark the curiosity in people to *want to* learn more, and *want to* communicate more. Our wish is that this will

help our Culturally community form meaningful human connections, and new friends for life.

Further to that, because the world is so interconnected now, it's easy to get on the next plane and fly to a foreign country, but how much of that time in a foreign place is spent communicating with and engaging with locals? When you book a walking tour in an effort to learn more, how much of your time is spent taking photos that you store in your camera or computer (which will never again see the light of day), instead of speaking to the people around you and learning about what makes their culture unique? Where is that tangible takeaway and real look into the authenticity of this new city you're in? That is why we built Culturally.

Participants at a New Zealand gin appreciation experience.

*Did you set out to create an experience in the field of cultural/experience? How did you do that?*
We did not set out to create our own experiences. Our belief was and is that there are so many amazingly talented and passionate cultural ambassadors out there, many of whom have years of experience behind them. Our platform should serve to promote them and bring their brand and what they have to offer to the rest of the world instead.

That said, we wanted the experiences on our platform to be unique, and more importantly, representative of our brand and vision to educate in order to connect. Therefore, we work with all our Culturally Ambassadors to ensure that the experiences they offer on our platform will always fulfil the criteria of being educational, hands-on and authentic.

We have a 152-point audit checklist that we go through with all our new and existing CAs every six months. This is to ensure we constantly optimize and ensure consistency in experience delivery amongst our offerings. The branding needs to be clear when you attend a Culturally workshop; you have learned something you never knew; you've experienced something tangible, and you've formed some sort of human connection through cultural education.

*Does your brand cater to the sharing economy? Or do you take the opposite route?*
Culturally focuses on bespoke workshops and experiences that are tailored to the demands and needs of our

consumers and corporate clients. The sharing economy implies (typically) underutilized assets or services shared. In the case of Culturally, a portion of our (culinary) experiences conducted by renowned local restaurants and bars are during their off-peak hours, but the assets delivered during this period are time, knowledge and materials. Such assets do not fall under those typically used in sharing economy transactions.

Whilst elements of our business model overlap with the principles underpinning business models operating in the sharing economy industry, we believe Culturally does not explicitly cater to the sharing economy.

Furthermore, the experiences (product) enjoyed by consumers who book on our platform are each and every one of them unique; because an experience is created not just by the tools and materials involved in the delivery of the experience, but more importantly by the people that participate and put their own special brand of flavour into each experience, thereby making it an even more bespoke brand experience!

*Has the arrival of social media and the sharing of experiences in these channels impacted your brand? Are you actively moulding your brand experiences to enable social media sharing?*
This is a tough question to answer. I think when our brand started, social media was already prevalent in the market and we knew that to hit the consumer market specifically, our branding had to be consistent and unique amongst all the other big travel players out there.

THE CULTURAL EXPERIENCE 99

Culturally team and Culturally Ambassadors at a sustainable woodworking experience.

Rallyer shows off her new handcrafted earrings.

Our #rallyer/attendees love taking photos when they are at our experiences. They love tagging friends and showing off the new ceramic vase or woodcut earrings they made. But the problem with being a platform is that consumers do not have the habit of wanting to tag you. You as the social platform are the medium, and even though without you, this experience would not have happened, consumers are consumed with the here and the now, which is the Culturally Ambassadors themselves, and whoever is participating in the workshop with them.

Because of that, we started implementing more measures to actively encourage interactions from customers and prospective customers on social media. Before a workshop and after a workshop, #rallyers receive an email from Culturally with useful information like nearby restaurants, tourist spots and opening hours, etc. The content of the email could also include best ways to take care of the new piece of indigo dyed cloth you've designed, or the recipe for the new dim sum dish you've learned to make. We have an ongoing monthly IG promo where #rallyers are incentivized to post a picture of their experience and tag us for a chance to win a free surprise workshop from Culturally. These and more ideas in the pipeline are how we hope to encourage more social media sharing of our brand experiences.

*Where do you see your brand in ten years?*
I would love for our brand to be a household name when people start talking about how to explore different cultures or how they made that amazing friend from *this*

The Peranakan heritage experience includes a talk on Peranakan artefacts and furniture as well as a hands-on session for participants to make their own *ondeh-ondeh* dessert.

A typesetting experience where you can learn how to use the different letters to create your own name or message and print out your creation.

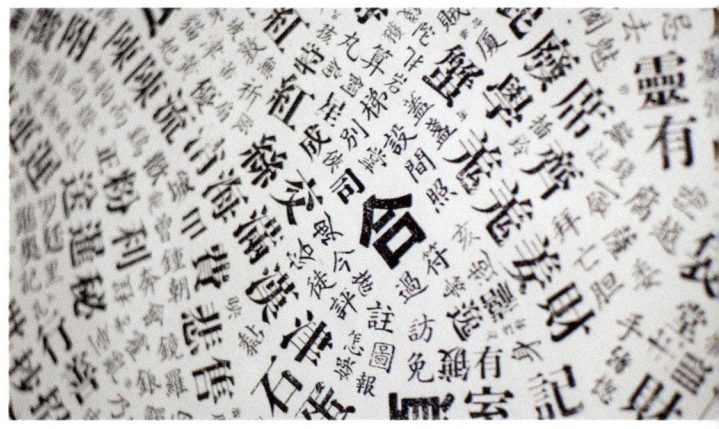

*place* on *that trip* during *that time*. I've made so many genuine friends from meeting #rallyers, or finding new Culturally Ambassadors. I truly want the rest of the world to be able to experience the same joy. Our platform is a technology platform, but we want to use technology to be the medium to catalyze the building of human connections in real life. We want to continue using technology to aid in the development and delivery of authentic experiences to induce human connections.

When people go to a foreign country, their first stop on the World Wide Web should be to Culturally's platform so that they can get a close in-depth introduction into another country's culture, meet a fellow musician, artist, potter, chef, horticulturist, etc. They can leave for home feeling like they've really engaged and learned something new culturally, and formed a real connection with another human being, instead of just having had a fun experience.

To help realise this ambition of a household name, we intend to set up brick-and-mortar experience centres, called "Culturally Houses" in the future. These outlets would showcase a range of global cultural experiences for visitors through smart technology, a hands-on approach and VR participation. We want our audience to experience different cultures around the world without the need to travel all over the world. These Culturally Houses will be in many cities around the world. We expect that a number of them could be attached to certain hotels as well. The main impact on branding behind such an initiative is to increase the connection that our audience has with our brand. People are always able to create a stronger relationship with a brand if they are able to interact with something tangible. Our Culturally Houses will be our agents for achieving this goal.

We also hope that in ten years' time, the Culturally brand becomes well-established amongst B2B clients. Good cross-cultural communication is crucial in the building of harmonious multicultural workforces. As multinational corporations (MNCs) become more diverse, they recognise cultural understanding and cultural empathy as key enablers in multicultural workforces. We hope that as each year passes, more MNCs will see the value of cultural experiences to their human resource missions and that the Culturally brand will play a key role in this trend. But more importantly, we will be able to deliver

Getting into costume is part of the fun in the Japanese tea appreciation experience.

in providing optimal experiences for teams to learn about one another's cultures and work together more effectively, with candour and respect.

### How to create a Cultural Experience
- Culture is local. So define your location first – either where you are (as a brand) or where you are taking people.
- Look into what is unique to the location. Often this has to do with skills such as the making of things manually before industrialization.
- If your brand is not just about cultural experiences themselves, find those that tie into your brand. This could be how it's made or where the ingredients come from. You'd already have access to the artisans.
- Make the experience hands-on. Give people something to do. Nothing is more satisfying than bringing something home that you made yourself.
- Make sure that the experience is unique to your brand and hard to find for any single traveller looking online. That way, they need to go through you.

CHAPTER 7

# THE SERVICE EXPERIENCE

> Recently, on a weekend in Tokyo, the weather was terrible – a big typhoon had just devastated the country, and rain was still coming down. During the 15-minute walk from the Metro station to my hotel at night, pulling my Rimowa with one hand and following Google Maps on the other, I got drenched. So when I arrived at the hotel reception, one staff started to check me in while another ran off, only to return a minute later with an armful of fluffy white towels so I could dry myself.

Good service is pre-emptive. It is based on an understanding of customers' needs, often before they themselves realise what their needs are. It can be formulaic to a certain extent (you don't want to depend fully on the employee's empathy or quick thinking), but

Sugar, the rooftop bar at EAST, Hong Kong.

a big part of it is spontaneous, by recognizing a gap, an opportunity to help or make an impression.

The rest of the trip continued along these lines, with friendly, unobtrusive service everywhere I went – from buying a ticket for my train to Kamakura to having my bowl filled with vegetables at the local shabu-shabu restaurant with a business associate.

The service experience is what you will remember – more than the price you paid, how the food tasted or the layout of your room. Great service is very hard to deliver because we are dealing with the biggest intangible: human beings.

That's why great service brands – in retail, hospitality, restaurants or travel – spend a lot of time and money to train their staff. It's what we call internal branding; people are an important touchpoint (because we are less forgiving of another person than of a machine that breaks down). They need to know what is expected of them, and

have detailed instructions on how to deliver the service. But most importantly, they need to buy into the brand and what it stands for, they need to be proud of their work and believe in its mission. We have become very good at seeing through the mask, and we can tell when service is genuinely friendly or staff are following the training manual with a fake smile. That's why telling our service staff what to do isn't enough. We need to treat them well, pay them well and develop them – in order to enable them to deliver a service that is genuine.

Singapore Airlines has for a long time represented good service – and to me it still does. But in comparison with other Asian airlines like Cathay Pacific (let's not even talk about Western airlines) their friendliness seemed somewhat learnt. People spoke about 'friendly robots'. It was all good, but very by the book. Good service is more than that – it is personal. The best service is based on a personal connection between the service provider and the customer. Singapore Airlines seem to have realised that, because recently I have been able to have a genuine conversation with the cabin crew, about the best places to eat in Singapore, or where to go for a drink in Bali.

In this book I am constantly encouraging the reader to go and try new things, new experiences, outside of the comfort zone. But the truth is, I am – just like you – a creature of habit. Once I've found the perfect restaurant, hotel or airline, I tend to be loyal. I know what to expect, and my loyalty is often rewarded. So after a few years of travel in Asia, I had my favourite hotels in most Asian capitals: The Metropolitan in Bangkok, The Legian in Bali, The Intercontinental in Manila (sadly demolished to make space for a parking lot), The Opposite House in Beijing, Andaz in Tokyo. Only in Hong Kong I kept trying out different hotel brands, partly because I lived there for three years and had no need for accommodation outside my tiny 51st floor apartment in Sheung Wan.

Then I discovered EAST. Maybe it was the location – off the beaten track in Tai Koo Shing, close to my old office in Tai Koo Fong, and to my friend Max's house so he could easily pop over for a meal or drink – that made me try it. But next to the hardware – great views over Victoria Harbour, spacious, clever rooms, a magnificent rooftop bar called Sugar – it was the service that made me return. From the check-in experience to dining at Feast, the amenities in the room and the welcome to the gym and heated pool, everywhere I went I experienced the same friendly and efficient, caring and proud service.

The stylish building facade speaks of the brand's enthusiasm and originality.

## Interview with Frances Mak, Area Communications Manager, Swire Hotels

*How would you describe, in one line, what your brand stands for?*
EAST is a place that's alive with enthusiasm, optimism and originality. Why the name EAST? This is where the sun rises and where every day begins. It is exactly this energy that we channel to create not just a hotel but a place where new ideas are born and get put into business.

*When and how was your brand started?*
The EAST brand started in 2010. It is the first lifestyle business hotel managed by Swire Hotels. Prior to EAST, Hong Kong, there was only The Opposite House in Beijing

and The Upper House in Hong Kong in our group which target mainly the luxury market. We wanted to create a totally new hotel concept for business travellers to choose from which is unfussy yet sophisticated in design and which provides a relaxing environment.

*When your brand was launched, what was the spark (as far as you know)? What were the consumer and market insights?*
Hong Kong has a lot of traditional business hotels in the market, but few targetted the young tech business traveller prior to the launch of our hotel. We understand the age group of the work force is changing. With the lifestyle of millenniasl in mind, we target to create a more fun and casual vibe for them on their business trips. This is a place when our guests need to get things done, it is plugged in for business; and when it's time to unwind or recharge, our guests will find the perfect uncluttered environment to relax.

*What were some of the challenges the brand faced over time?*
Swire Hotels is all about cutting-edge design, fun, quality and good value, which was a quite a new concept when we opened in 2009. With more lifestyle hotels opening since then, the competition has become very fierce and being able to stay strong in the market has become a one of the biggest challenges.

Keeping up with the latest technology trends is another big challenge for us but it is essential for the hotel industry, because the industry itself is extremely competitive. We have been putting our best effort in upgrading our technology since who fails to adapt can quickly find that they are left behind by hotel and travel companies that have implemented new approaches and ideas.

*What's the one brand story you have been telling over and over?*
EAST is a business playground that's carefully designed for the go-getting urbanite. Whether our audiences are travellers or locals in the city, we seek to offer them an invigorating experience where they can mix work and play seamlessly.

*Your brand is known for excellent service. Did you set out to create an experience in the field of service? How did you do that?*
We build an entirely new service culture which is all about delivering wonderful personal service and attention to our guests. EAST is about people. We value our people and treat them very well so they enjoy working with us. They are energetic and passionate about understanding our guests and what they need.

*In a segment where service is paramount, can it still work as a differentiator? How?*
We focus on guests' needs and provide additional personalised and extraordinary service depending on their actual requirements. People nowadays are concerned about value for money, therefore we keep our service and

*Top*: Main entrance of the hotel at night.
*Bottom*: Function room in a banquet and ceremony setup.

*Top*: Guestrooms are furnished in a stylish yet cosy manner.
*Bottom*: Suites offer impressive views of the city.

standard high with fantastic value for money. Our only directive is to make our guests' stay as enjoyable as they can. This certainly will be a visible differentiator for our targeted guests.

*Do you find your guests' expectations of service have changed? How?*
A lot of guests, especially the younger travellers, are looking for a lifestyle hotel that is unpretentious and down to earth yet fun to stay in with big attention to details. EAST is a lifestyle hotel for those who are looking for the perfect uncluttered environment to relax, unwind or recharge.

*Has the arrival of social media and the sharing of experiences in these channels impacted your brand? Are you actively moulding your brand experiences to enable social media sharing?*
Thanks to the popularity of social media, our signature rooms became well-known within the online community. Hence, we received quite a few enquiries via the internet and social platforms. The other way round, social media also allows us to reach out to our target audience more effectively through demographic and other settings. We are able to create hashtags and campaigns to interact with online users, as well as making our social media account names noticeable within the premises of hotel, pre-arrival email and promotion posters, etc, to maximise our brand online presence.

*Where do you see your brand in ten years?*
We see increasing demand not just for hotels but for multi-purpose places where people can work productively and have fun and get inspired at the same time. This is exactly the kind of need that EAST is dedicated to, so we see a great deal of potential for our brand, here in Hong Kong and in more cities around the world.

### How to create a Service Experience
- People like people. Make sure you train and motivate your staff to deliver a genuine friendliness.
- Service is personal. Remember names and preferences of customers.
- Service needs structure. Don't hesitate to develop a rule book to make sure the experience is consistent.
- Service needs to be quick. Empower your staff by giving them the responsibility (and budget) to make fast decisions to help a customer
- Service can be recovered. If something goes wrong, be transparent, apologetic and generous.

CHAPTER 8

# THE DIGITAL EXPERIENCE

> Digital has changed our lives and continues to change it. This has an impact on many other touchpoints for our brands, from shopfronts to people (less personal interaction), pricing to brand collaborations (with delivery companies who suddenly become part of our brand experience).

Just having an online presence isn't enough any more. There are different ways to build this presence and different levels of user-friendliness. The digital experience we create makes a big difference to how our overall brand is being perceived. Many big brands can tell you stories about how some bug in the algorithm or a too-slow booking experience led to an outcry by customers. This is another thing that has changed. Customers now have a voice, at least in the digital realm, and any sub-par experience will without doubt lead to angry write-ups on Facebook,

TripAdvisor or any other online portal. This in turn influences potential customers who tend to believe reviews more than messages that come directly from the brand.

Fundamentally, creating a fulfilling digital brand experience needn't be difficult; it starts, like any brand experience, from an understanding of the target group and their needs. How are they using your website? Is it for browsing, information and inspiration or for a quick-in-and-out shopping transaction? Are they looking for quality or price or both? The answers should give you some pointers about the structure of your website. Does it have a call to action? Does your Instagram profile have a button that says "Shop here"?

If there was one word used to describe the main advantage that the internet – from social media to shopping sites, news to travel, traffic to ride-share booking – offers, it is convenience. Having our smartphone with us just makes life so much easier – from finding information in discussions with our friends, staying in touch with old schoolmates, finding hidden addresses, organizing getting from A to B. So this should be the guiding light for the online experience you create. Make it convenient for people.

In digital branding as in anywhere else, know your target group. Understand what they are looking for online, then deliver that experience to them. Are you offering information? Convenience? Education? Entertainment? Or a combination of all? The fact is that people are not looking for ads online. So you'd better deliver some kind of value that is relevant to them. An interesting field to explore is online content. Content is information, education or entertainment which is not directly trying to sell your brand – but is connected to your brand in a meaningful way. That connection cannot be too weak (when any other brand can be added at the end of the video, people are likely to remember the content but not your brand), but neither can it be too strong (then the perception of the content piece is that it is an advertisement and it is easily overlooked or dismissed).

At Audi, when we were looking to raise awareness for and position our 4-wheel-drive system, "quattro", my content team in the global HQ discovered a French skier, Candide Thovex, who had a big following online for his videos where he skied on different surfaces. "This is perfect," they said. "All conditions are perfect conditions for Candide and for the Audi quattro." After the initial video which showed him going downhill on grass to land in the boot of an Audi Q7, we developed an ambitious plan for Candide and the team to go around the world and shoot skiing stunts on all sort of different materials: from sand to walls (the Great Wall of China, no less), water to rocks. I remember showing the storyboard to my boss just before an Audi Cup football match at Munich's Allianz Stadium. "I like it," he said, "but where is my brand?" We explained to him that the brand was in the logo in the skies, and super-imposed on the image at the beginning and the end of the video where we'd make the connection between all conditions and quattro. "No cars?" he asked. "No cars," we said. But then we decided to build one sand Audi in a scene where Candide goes past some children playing on the beach. It's there, but when you blink, you miss it.

Here lies the beauty of content – if you manage to find a topic that interests people (because it is novel and exciting) and manage to create a strong messaging link to your brand (all conditions are perfect conditions), you don't need to show your product too much. You can keep that for the 'behind the scenes' video. The Candide/quattro series received millions of views and won us a few Lions at the advertising festival in Cannes in 2018.

Remember the days when you had to find the phone number of the restaurant you wanted to go to (where are the Yellow Pages?), call them up (why is nobody answering the phone?), reserve, then make your way there hoping for a good dining experience? Restaurant booking platforms like Chope have changed all this, both for customers and restaurateurs. With one easy app you can now (conveniently) find the restaurant you're looking for and reserve a table – often with some special deal that comes with it.

**2011**  **2012–2015**  **2015–2016**  **2016–2018**  **March 2019**

Chope's logo over the years.

**Interview with Kunal Narang, Regional General Manager, Indonesia & Thailand, Chope.**

*How would you describe, in one line, what your brand stands for?*
Chope strives to connect billions of diners with millions of restaurants in Asia in whichever way possible, starting with online reservations. We focus on in-restaurant services to provide better experiences in order to encourage society to get out, be social and connect with one another over food.

*When and how was your brand started?*
Chope was started in 2011, in Singapore. Since then it has entered other markets such as Jakarta, Bali, Bangkok, Phuket, Hong Kong and Shanghai.

*When your brand was launched, what was the spark (as far as you know)? What were the consumer and market insights?*
Since we started in Singapore, people connected to the slang word "chope" which in Singapore traditionally meant to informally reserve your seat in a busy area by placing a small personal belonging on the seat. This culture was most prevalent in the local hawker centers so food was very much part of how people related to the word "chope". Today we work with more than 4,000 restaurants across the region and while "chope" may not have the same meaning in the other markets outside Singapore we are in, we have found that users across the

board see us as a fun, energetic, young brand. Perhaps it has to do with our colour theme of yellow. Our logo has evolved over the years as well a few times. Most recently, we changed our logo in 2019 after our first full rebranding exercise was done.

*What were some of the challenges the brand faced over time?*

Speaking for myself, I started a company called MakanLuar.com in 2013 which I then sold to Chope in 2016. At the beginning of a fresh company, it was based on theoretically how big we could make this one day and how fun would it be for everyone involved, how we are bringing something new to the market. As the company matured, we started needing more than just the founders' vision for the brand. We started to need inputs from all stakeholders involved in terms of what does the company and its services represent to customers and employees. Those are the two key parts of the equation making the whole thing work. It became increasingly important to understand why customers continue to use us, why employees like coming to work everyday.

2016    2017    2018    2019

Diners' Choice evolution over the years.

I remember at one point we had about 10 to 15 management team members in a room talking about what the brand meant to us and what we felt it represented. While there were some similar underlying themes, many of the views were quite different too. That's when we realised we needed to re-invest, re-invent, re-question the brand's values and why we are working on what we are working on to re-align all of us again across all stakeholders to our central mission.

*How has the brand changed over time? What prompted these changes, and were they proactive or reactive?*
I feel much of this may have been addressed by the previous question. In general some of it was reactive; however, the reactive elements triggered a broader discussion into the larger meaning behind the brand, which was proactive. Often we don't take certain steps until we are able to experience some of the pain-points. However, once we commit to solving those pain-points, we aim to address some foreseeable related pain-points proactively.

*What's the one brand story you have been telling over and over?*
We are fun, we are social, we aim to provide great value for memorable experiences when dining out.

*Did you set out to create an experience in the field of apps/online booking systems? How did you do that?*
Chope was started by Arrif Ziaudeen questioning "Why Not?" He had spent time in the US and seen similar

services out there so when he came back to Singapore, he questioned why such services were not available for dining out in most of Asia. Hence if someone was going to do it, then "Why Not" him?

Similarly when I started MakanLuar.com, I knew someone would end up building a platform to connect diners to restaurants the way we do, so in essence the motivation for me was the same, "Why Not" me?

We started off by researching how similar models worked in other parts of the world, we spoke to a number of restaurants to understand their processes, existing services and competing tools they were using and built from there. Technology adoption from both merchants and users in some markets can be slower than others, hence the brand mission and values are key to driving it forward as one unit across the company.

*Does your brand cater to the sharing economy? Or do you take the opposite route?*

We are an asset-light model in that we are not running our own restaurants or building physical infrastructure for restaurants. We are purely a technology services company, which enables us to scale quickly. With that said, we are not part of the sharing economy in the modern sense of using "gig"-based orders through a freelance/part-time worker network as our core way of doing things. We have full-time employees dedicated to providing our service through in-house resources and controls.

We are, however, part of the sharing economy in the sense that we help provide consumers a service which

Chope's 8th birthday - use of stamps, slanted text, device holders in line with the new branding.

adds value to their dining experience. What we do enables them to share memorable, social moments with others – friends, family, colleagues, clients, partners or anyone else.

*Has the arrival of social media and the sharing of experiences in these channels impacted your brand? Are you actively moulding your brand experiences to enable social media sharing?*

Absolutely. The company was born in an era when social media was already prevalent. The social media landscape has since evolved quickly and continues to move at lightning speed. Social media is one of our key platforms to communicate with our community of diners, restaurants, industry members and even for public relations purposes. We have been actively encouraging sharing of moments that we are part of for consumers on social media via a wide array of campaigns for a number of years now.

2018

2019

Secret Angpao Campaign – 2018 vs 2019.

*Where do you see your brand in ten years?*
We have recently done our re-brand exercise for the long term and we hope that the brand continues to represent the same mission and values in another ten years, at a wider, more impactful scale. This vision is to connect billions of diners with millions of restaurants in Asia by helping consumers add value to their dining experience, to enable sharing memorable, social moments with others.

### How to build a Digital Experience
- Don't complicate or overthink things. The best platforms are easy to use.
- Keep your customer in mind. What are they looking for from your digital presence? Deliver that first, then you can add more options or services.
- How can you make their lives easier? Don't think about what you offer but what they need for a great holistic experience. It is not just a table in a restaurant but maybe parking/transport, an advance menu or a welcome drink.
- Think twice before you create an app. An app only makes sense if you have enough supply to become a one-stop-shop, or if you are a monopoly. Otherwise, invest in an easy (mobile-enabled) website.
- Don't look at digital in isolation. How does it work together with your brick-and-mortar shops? How does it deliver the same consistent experience as your service?

CHAPTER 9

# THE OVERALL BRAND EXPERIENCE

> Students in my Strategic Brand Management classes learn that above all branding steps, three points are the most important: your brand needs to be relevant (to the consumer), differentiated (from the competition) and consistent (across touchpoints, channels and borders).

So why a chapter on the overall brand experience? Many brands have a big number of touchpoints (not all controlled by marketing) that nevertheless contribute to the brand impression. That's why it is important to think about the experience we create holistically. Unfortunately, we often don't – because that's not how we work. Due to size and/or specialization, we often work in silos where one department is looking at shopfronts, one at the product, another does advertising, and often there is a separate digital department. Even the third-party

The entrance of Straits Clan from Bukit Pasoh Road.

support that we hire, in the form of agencies, works in its specialized fields.

From a consumer point of view, however, they see one brand. They don't care whether the uniforms are developed by human resource, the invoice is sent by finance, the Instagram page is created by marketing. To them it is all the same brand, and the message, story, look and feel should be consistent. If they aren't, customers often get confused and potentially start doubting the brand: "You are telling me you are the friendly brand, but my own experience with your shop staff is different, so I don't believe you."

That's why I thought it would be good to find an example of a brand that has managed to create a consistent experience across all touchpoints. Fifteen years ago, when I was working in Hong Kong, I happened to join a private member's club, KEE Club, on top of a famous roast goose restaurant (Yung Kee) in Wellington Street in Central. The club was quirky and cosy, offered excellent lunch and dinner and was the perfect place to meet friends after work, celebrate pre-wedding dinners (as I did) and ignore the visiting and local celebrities.

Returning to Singapore, I looked for a similar club but couldn't find one. The existing clubs were too rigid, too formal for me. It took another ten years before I heard about the New Majestic Hotel being converted into a private members' club, the Straits Clan. I reached out to the management, got a tour of the construction site by Aun Koh, and joined as a Founding Member. Because what I saw was exactly the eclectic mix of old and new, traditional and modern, high quality with quirky ideas, that I was looking for.

The execution of the brand did not disappoint – from collaborations with local artists to the menu in the restaurant, networking nights to the members app, controversial discussions to happening parties. Every single touchpoint has been carefully crafted to portray the essence of the brand.

The bar at Straits Clan.

**Interview with Cynthia Salim, Director: Content & Community, Straits Clan.**

*How would you describe, in one line, what your brand stands for?*
Straits Clan is a members' club where a community of progressive thought-leaders, inspired by a dynamic roster of best-in-class content, come together to do more and do better.

*When and how was your brand started?*
Straits Clan opened its doors in May 2018, but the foundations of the brand were laid a few years prior, before any of the real work began.

"My journey as an entrepreneur has given me the incredible opportunity to work with many progressive creatives, business leaders, and change-makers across numerous fields in the last decade," says co-founder Wee Teng Wen. The impetus to create a space for genuine connection between change-makers from different fields led Wee Teng Wen and his co-founders, Aun Koh and Sally Sim, to build Straits Clan.

The co-founders aligned around a shared vision of creating a private members' club that sought to challenge what a traditional members' club stood for, one that wasn't based on wealth or status, but on passions. One that celebrated the way people in this part of the world liked to work, live and play. The hope was that Straits Clan would ultimately showcase the sense of place – Singapore as a cosmopolitan city with a confluence of cultures and a hub for boundary-pushing ideas.

*When your brand was launched, what was the spark (as far as you know)? What were the consumer and market insights?*

It's truly an exciting time for Singapore. The creative and entrepreneurial zeal here is palpable. We have many passionate individuals working on great ideas, great social issues, though all arguably in silos with very little opportunity to cross-pollinate. There is currently no central gathering place in Singapore for people to meet and cultivate relationships with likeminded individuals from different backgrounds.

The stylish and inviting Clan Cafe is also open to the public.

*What were some of the challenges the brand faced over time?*
The duality of being a club that represents diversity and inclusion in a world that by all definitions is exclusive. Diversity in our desire not just for member representation, but also in the nature of our offering and the content line-up we curated. It was and continues to be this delicate balance of listening to our members, while ensuring we aren't bending to those with louder voices.

THE OVERALL BRAND EXPERIENCE    137

Madam Wong's is an intimate space for karaoke sessions.

*How has the brand changed over time? What prompted these changes, and were they proactive or reactive?*
At Straits Clan's inception, the visual and verbal language the brand adopted was intentionally discreet, a little more shrouded in mystery, arguably learning from the communication strategies of its Western counterparts. Over time, the brand has evolved to be a lot more open and vibrant, based on our understanding of the local landscape and consumer perceptions. There was much

Sample the best from different distilleries at the Whisky Bar.

misconception surrounding a new age members' club – its value, its intention – so much so adopting a closed-door communication approach was doing the brand no favours.

*How does the brand express itself? More through the building or the programmes, the staff or the members?*
The Straits Clan, at its core, is about a community of progressive, passionate individuals and our ability

to inspire each one of them to be the best versions of themselves. This manifests in all three tenets: our community, our content, and our culture. The brand is at its best self when all three ebb and flow in perfect harmony. We've always said that the best experience at Straits Clan is one in which you come for an event you ordinarily might not have signed up for (one that surprises you pleasantly in its ability to challenge your world view). At this event, you end up meeting other members, one of whom you really bond with due to a shared passion, which you decide to pursue together. All the while in a safe haven that feels like your home away from home.

*What's the one brand story you have been telling over and over?*
The name 'Straits Clan' takes inspiration from clan associations that were a core part of Singapore's social fabric in the 19th century. In a city of immigrants, individuals sought comfort and kinship in their clan. Over time, what started out as friendship became catalysts for social change in the wider community with clans championing societal advancements in education, infrastructure, and commerce.

Located on Bukit Pasoh Road, once known as the Street of Clans, our club resides within a heritage-listed building in Singapore's historic Chinatown district. It pays tribute to generations past in celebrating the spirit of community and a thirst for change. We hope this will be the start of something good; the start of better, more beautiful things to come.

*Top*: A typical event set-up at Straits Clan.
*Bottom left*: Actress Lucy Liu speaking on her exhibition, Unhomed Belongings.
*Bottom right*: A session with Dominique Crenn, the only female chef in America to attain three Michelin stars for her restaurant, Atelier Crenn.

*Top*: French writer and Buddhist monk Matthieu Ricard shares his wisdom.
*Bottom*: Pia Leon, voted Latin America's Best Female Chef 2018, does a dining takeover.

*Did you set out to create an experience in the field of private members' clubs? How did you do that?*
Yes. By focusing on our pillars of community, content and culture with equal fervour. And by continuously listening to our members and improving along the way.

*Does your brand cater to the sharing economy? Or do you take the opposite route?*
The content programme at Straits Clan is, at its core, a democratisation of knowledge.

*Has the arrival of social media and the sharing of experiences in these channels impacted your brand?*
*Are you actively moulding your brand experiences to enable social media sharing?*
To combat the lack of awareness of such a new world social club in Singapore, we leveraged our social platforms and the current #FOMO culture to build a deeper understanding and interest in what we were striving to create.

*Where do you see your brand in ten years?*
As a one-year-old venture, Straits Clan is primarily focused on improving the member experience. In ten years, however, we hope to have become an integral component of the society in which we operate, much like the clans of our forefathers.

## How to build your Overall Brand Experience

- Branding is more than marketing. That's why it should be anchored with the CEO's office, otherwise the other departments won't follow.
- Sit down and think of all points where the consumer touches the brand. There are more than you think. Then decide how each touchpoint expresses your brand.
- Look at brands that you want or need to collaborate with, everything from food to delivery. They are your touchpoints, too – consumers often don't differentiate.
- Enable your customers as they can be your brand ambassadors. Give them stories to tell, creating word-of-mouth exposure, and keep them loyal.
- Think merchandise. What is appropriate to tell your brand story and can bring the logo where no other logo can go?

CHAPTER 10

# EXPERIENCES AND CULTURAL MOMENTS

So experiences can help you differentiate your brand – they can help position it, convey its story and communicate how it is different from the competition. They can also help to personalize the brand by creating something unique that is very relevant to the person engaging with it. Experiences are something that your target audience will remember, good or bad – no matter how many times advertising will try to convince us (with a big amount of money spent for the effort) that Brand A is a friendly brand; once we have a bad phone experience with their customer service we will remember it forever, and tell all our friends about it.

We trust our own experiences more than any announcements from brands, however fancy they may be. But if it's a good experience, one that not only positions the brand but also ourselves (as adventurous, discerning, caring, daring, clever, sophisticated – the list is endless), then we will use all our social media channels plus word-of-mouth to share it with our friends, thus increasing the brand's reach.

Oh, and talking about reach: sometimes we don't even have to create the experience from scratch but can hop on the bandwagon of an existing phenomenon. We call this Cultural Moments. Every culture has its own, and some are shared globally. Would you agree that Christmas can be an amazing experience? Or the family gatherings during Lunar New Year, Hari Raya or Deepavali?

Brands can use the attention that these cultural moments are already getting as an elevator to the top, to borrow awareness by some clever association. In Singapore, for the country's 50th National Day a few years ago, dozens of brands were using the "SG50" logo to connect their brand to the moment, hoping to benefit from the goodwill and attention of the public. On Mother's Day (celebrated on different days in different markets, which makes it a nightmare for global marketers), films retell stories of a mother's love for her children, or vice versa, and how their brand has played a part in it.

On a Wednesday afternoon in early 2018, in a conference room in Munich airport, our Hamburg agency thjnk presented campaign ideas for some upcoming car launches to me and my Audi team. After they were done, and we were ready to pack up and drive back to our Ingolstadt HQ, their creative director said: "Wait. There's one more thing."

And they presented some ideas for an upcoming Cultural Moment: 24th June 2018, when women in Saudi Arabia would be allowed to drive for the first time. Amongst the handful of ideas presented, we liked one simple one best:

A Saudi Arabian couple are getting ready to leave their house. As they pass through a series of doors in the big mansion, the husband opens every single one of them for his wife, allowing her to pass through first. Finally, they reach the courtyard where an Audi S5 is parked. They both walk to the car. She reaches it a second before him, opens the passenger door for him, inviting him with a smile and a nod of the head to get into the passenger seat. She then sits in the driver's seat and they drive away. The super-imposed text reads: "It is time to open more doors. Audi welcomes the women of Saudi Arabia to the driver's seat."

We immediately saw the potential of the ad, in positioning the brand as 'progressive' and tapping into this moment, but also the dangers. If not done correctly, we could be accused of using their achievement for commercial purposes, we could even end up with an online shitstorm, the last thing we needed as a brand.

So I had to make sure we got this right. I sent the script to my colleagues in Dubai (who loved it) and asked them to check with the office in Riyadh (who also loved it). Then I asked our Middle Eastern colleagues to be involved in the shoot, making sure that it would look authentic – from casting of the talent, to styling, the house, the street, the music. Everybody worked together and we were able to produce a touching online film which we launched on our social media channels a few days before the actual event. The echo was overwhelming and almost 100% positive. Why? Because we did not make this about us. The film was not trying to sell cars. It was celebrating a cultural, political achievement. But there was an obvious

A photo showing a woman at the wheel of a car. It is from Audi's advertisement campaign in Saudi Arabia to mark the landmark ruling permitting women in the country to drive.

connection between the cultural moment and our product (it was about driving) and our brand (it was a progressive statement). I remember many people in my team, and also my boss, being skeptical at first. But sometimes you need to take the plunge (after making sure all safeguards are in place). The online experience we created really helped our brand and shone a spotlight on the cultural moment for months after it had passed. Of all the materials I was responsible for during my six years with the car brand, this is the one I am most proud of.

## ABOUT THE AUTHOR

Photo by Jazpar Yeo

**Jörg Dietzel** grew up in Germany and was educated at the University of Bonn, Germany, and the University of Natal, Durban, South Africa. After training as a journalist, he started working in advertising, first in Germany, then London, Beijing, Singapore and Hong Kong. He ran DDB China and founded DDB Berlin, was Chief Development Officer for the legendary Batey Ads agency in Singapore (who invented the Singapore Girl for SIA). In 2005, he started his own brand consultancy in Singapore and was asked to teach at the National University of Singapore and the Singapore Management University (SMU). In 2013, his former client offered him the position of Director of Marketing at Audi Korea in Seoul, followed by two years as global Head of Creative and Sales Media at Audi's HQ in Ingolstadt, Germany. In 2019 Jörg returned to Singapore, his home of choice, where he teaches Advertising and Strategic Brand Management at SMU, consults clients, gives talks and workshops on branding and hosts programmes on TV and radio.